Denis Alphonsus Quinn

Ireland in '89,

Or, a Brief History of Ireland from the Union to the Present Day

Denis Alphonsus Quinn

Ireland in '89,
Or, a Brief History of Ireland from the Union to the Present Day

ISBN/EAN: 9783337124182

Printed in Europe, USA, Canada, Australia, Japan

Cover: Foto ©ninafisch / pixelio.de

More available books at **www.hansebooks.com**

EVICTION OF MR. CLEARY AND FAMILY FROM HOMESTEAD ON THE VANDELEUR ESTATE, KILRUSH, CO. CLARE. FIRST STROKE OF THE BATTERING RAM, (BALFOUR'S MAIDEN) 1889.

IRELAND IN '89,

OR,

A BRIEF HISTORY OF IRELAND FROM THE UNION TO THE PRESENT DAY,

TO WHICH IS ADDED

A GRAPHIC SKETCH OF IRISH SCENERY, MINSTRELSY AND CHARACTER.

BY ZENO.

"*And nations have fallen, and thou still art young,
Thy sun is but rising when others are set:
And tho' slavery's gloom o'er thy morning hath hung
A full moon of freedom shall beam 'round thee yet.*"

MOORE.

PROVIDENCE, R. I.
E. L. FREEMAN & SON, PRINTERS.
1889.
COPYRIGHT 1890 BY REV. D. A. QUINN.

TO THE READER.

Judging from the ever increasing tide of ornate superficial literature that threatens to inundate the present age, a disinterested observer would naturally suppose the writers merely intended to please the eye, and to palm polished paper, elaborate typography and artistic binding, a substitute for interesting facts or fiction.

Writers of all ages, especially of the present, might be compared to two species of well-known insects; butterflies and ants. The butterflies are indeed beautiful creatures, charming the eye as they flit from flower to flower, basking in the sunshine and sipping sweets which they did not make themselves; the ants, on the contrary, whilst being unseemly creatures, are tiny embodiments of thrift; they never purloin the fruit of other insects' labor, and their little homes, however humble, are the creation of their own industry.

The Author respectfully begs to be classified with the latter. If the subsequent pages do not reveal a wealth of talents, they are at least innocent of plagiarism; everything that has been borrowed is carefully labeled with the author's name or the source from which it emanated.*

In subscribing a *nom de plume*, instead of our patronymic, we merely wished to divorce ourselves from every patronage which relatives or religion might invest in a name.

---

*The Author begs to state that during the past year he has conversed with several Irish Representatives and witnessed many of the events he described.

If this little volume does not suit the popular taste, we have only to regret that the public appetite is indisposed to receive our humble offering.

As a mother often fails to gratify the gustatory organs of her children, after they have already been satiated with coarser viands, so the Author does not expect to be able to please the capricious tastes of all, especially of those who have already been glutted with more solid literature.

We are prepared to hear many of our male and female patrons poutingly disparage the promiscuous *deserts* of our unpretending literary refreshments; wishing they contained fewer *bitter* things, more *ardent* stimulants and *saccharine* ingredients.

However, since it is not an individual or group of individuals, but a proscribed nation we have undertaken to *serve*, and in trying to furnish the inhabitants with what they most desire, have exercised our best endeavors, we hope the reader will appreciate—perhaps applaud our efforts. Z.

Providence, R. I., Feb. 22d, 1890.

CHAPTER I.

A BIRD'S-EYE-VIEW OF THE GEOGRAPHY, CLIMATE AND NATURAL RESOURCES OF IRELAND.

THIS prolific but unprosperous motherland of exiles, dispersed throughout every habitable country of the globe, possesses patent advantages of climate, topography and soil, over every nation of Europe; whilst no Australian colony, or American State or Territory can compare with it in physical resources.

The temperature of Ireland seldom rises above 75, or descends lower than 30 degrees Fahr., whilst Manitoba (Canada) in the same, or nearly the same latitude, has but two seasons, winter and summer. Moscow is much colder during the months of winter and spring, while the Ural mountains of Russia, in lower latitude, are perennially snow-capped.

Those geographic lines that divide zones and hemispheres do not always indicate climate or temperature.

Ireland and the British Isles owe their mild temperature to some other influence, perhaps to that of the Gulfstream, rather than to their geographical position.

In the map of the world, Ireland lies between 51° 26′ and 55° 21′ N. Lat., and 5° 26′ and 10° 29′ W. Long.

Its adjacency to Great Britain is commercially important, the distance from Kingston to Holyhead being only 64 miles, whilst Fortpatrick in Scotland is but $21\frac{1}{2}$ miles from Donoughadee in Ireland. The country is divided into four provinces which are subdivided into 32 counties, of which twelve belong to Leinster in the East, nine to Ulster in the North, six to Munster in the South and five to Connaught in the West. On account of their political union and physical proximity, Ireland, England and Scotland have sometimes been called "sister kingdoms." The Maid of Erin, however, has always disclaimed this alleged consanguinity, justly regarding the Lion and Unicorn as of different genesis and gender.

The extreme length of Ireland, from Fair Head in Antrim, to Mizen Head in Cork, is about 300 miles; and its breadth from Howth Head in Dublin to Slyne Head in Galway is about 170 miles; its area, comprising 32,524 sq. miles, (of which 711 are water) is 516 sq. miles less than the State of Maine. Its highest mountain is 3,414 feet above the level of the sea; and its largest river (the Shannon) is 254 miles long; its largest lake (Lough Neagh) covers a surface of 98,255 acres.

The Irish harbors are amongst the most commodious and finest in the world; of these, fourteen are capable of holding the largest ships afloat; it possesses about the same number sufficiently deep for frigates, and from thirty to forty suitable for any purpose of commerce. Whilst Liverpool is 3,016 miles from New York, the cable distance from this latter port to Queenstown is only 2,726 miles; Galway harbor is still more favorably situated, being but 2,371 miles distant from New York, and 1656 miles from St. John's (Newfoundland), a trip any of our modern ocean racers could finish in or about three days. The patent odds of 290 miles which nature has allotted to Queenstown and 645 miles to Galway, (19 and 49 hours ordinary sailing) are advantages which merchants and mariners cannot fail to appreciate.

In stormy weather, the passage of the St. George's channel is frequently more harassing to emigrants and tourists than the entire voyage across the Atlantic. As a majority of those who succumb to sea-sickness continue so until they leave the ship or steamer, those who embark at Queenstown escape, during 18 or 20 hours, this nauseous affliction. Moreover, the dense fog which frequently overspreads the waters between England and Ireland often incites the maledicent capabilities of sailors and sea-captains.

Although its seems paradoxical, what enhances the commercial and social condition of other nations appears to militate against the prosperity of Ireland and the Irish people. During the past half or whole century, the progress of civilization and growth of foreign and domestic industry have not only magnified, but created great cities and commercial depots in other countries. It has been otherwise, if not the contrary, with Ireland.

Before we refer to the decline of its commerce and agriculture, it will be pertinent to examine the popular statistics.

In 1821, the population of Ireland was a fraction less than 7,000,000; in 1845, it reached its highest estimate, 8,174,124. Ever since, the population has gradually decreased. In 1851, the figures fell down to 6,552,385; in 1861, 5,795,564; in 1881, 5,174,836; at present, (1889) the population of Ireland does not exceed four and a half millions. Ever since the famine and failure of the potato crop, in '45 and '46, Ireland's population has decreased over three and a half million (almost 40 per cent). From May, 1851, to the end of December, '85, no fewer than 3,051,351 persons of both sexes and all ages emigrated from Irish shores; in 1883, 105,743 left, whilst ever since, up to the present year (1889) an average of 62,000 persons annually leave Ireland, of whom, the greater number, wend their way to the United States. Ireland, though possessing numerous natural advantages over the so-called sister kingdoms, is far beneath them in her exhibition of agriculture, manufacture and commerce. That the commutative industries of Ireland at the present day are pinioned, if not completely paralyzed, does not appear to be an overstrained allegation.

CHAPTER II.

AT the consummation of the "Union" in 1800-1801, Ireland was an important factor of the British Empire. Ireland's place in the national economy, at present, is very discouraging. Whilst England and Wales contribute to the national exchequer £26,651,999, Ireland's contribution is but £1,995,550. In the whole Island, there are but two cities (Dublin and Belfast) that are of any commercial importance. Indeed, whilst Belfast has amazingly progressed, all other important cities of Ireland have noticeably retrograded. Belfast, being the stronghold of Orangeism, owes its prosperity to the direct subsidy and sympathy of the British Government. The lakes and rivers of Ireland abound with fish; but this source of wealth is almost entirely neglected; its mineral resources are abundant, and yet they have degenerated; its cattle and cereal productions should be trebly increased before the country could be considered in a normal condition. Scotland, whose barren plains and heather mountains were unnoticed by the eyes of the world of trade and traffic three quarters of a century ago, with a comparative scant population (1,625,000) has at present more than four million inhabitants, and will probably, in less than a year hence, exceed that of Ireland. The Irish Liberator, Daniel O'Connell, gave a painful description of Ireland, in his day. He was appealing for a *real*, and not a parchment "Union" when he spoke as follows:

"England and Ireland have too long answered to the fable of the dwarf and giant, where the dwarf gets all the blows and the giant comes in for all the honor and plunder. Now, I tell you we will not endure that Ireland should be the dwarf by the side of such a giant power as England! but raise her political standard to the stature of England and Scotland, and then—hurrah for the Union. For six hundred years the iron hoof of misrule has trampled upon the green isle of my lovely land. Her soil is fertile to exuberance, for no summer sun scorches it to sterility, nor does the winter chill it into barrenness—fertile to exuberance are her valleys— lovely are her rivers as they rush from the sides of her mountains and flow through her green plains—oh! not to bear on their bosoms the products of her commerce— would to Heaven it were; but exporting from her the very necessaries of life, while their banks are lined with a starving people. Her harbors are safe from every gale and open at every hour of every tide, and yet, though a solitary sail may occasionally be seen on her seas, commerce she has none. Her sons wander over every land as the accursed of Heaven, and they are to be found in every country toiling for that subsistence which is denied them at home, supported in their exile only by the exuberance of their native spirits, and sighing in secret sorrow that they shall never more behold the land of their birth. Why is Ireland without commerce?—Misgovernment. Why is she without manufactures?—Misgovernment. Why are her sons starving among fields that teem with produce?—Misgovernment. I call upon you to rid your souls of the curse of acquiescing in this mischief. I shall carry back to my country a tale of joy. I shall tell my countrymen that I read in the countenances of the manly, shrewd, and determined people of Scotland a determination to join us in struggling for our rights. I shall tell them that a nation never exceeded in the arts of war and in the bravery of her sons—I shall tell them that a country which, in the words of one of our countrymen who was an orator, soars in the full blaze of the arts and sciences 'with an eye that never winks and a wing that never tires'—that you have vowed, and I now vow for you—Ireland shall be free."

Dean Swift, writing of Ireland, said, "It is the poorest of all civilized countries, with every advantage to make it one of the greatest." Lord Dufferin, when governor of India in '67, held similar views: "Some human agency must be accountable for the perennial desolation of a lovely and fertile land, watered by the fairest streams; caressed by a clement atmosphere; held in the embrace of a sea, whose affluence fills the richest harbors in the world; and inhabited by a race, valiant, tender, generous and gifted beyond measure with the power of physical endurance and blessed with the liveliest intelligence." The London "Times" once admitted that all the famines and financial depressions that occurred in Ireland were artificial. Lord Dufferin again wrote: "From Queen Elizabeth's reign (that is from 1600 to 1800) the various commercial confraternities of Great Britain never for a moment relaxed their relentless grasp on the trades and manufactures of Ireland. One by one, each of our nascent industries were either strangled in its birth, or handed over, gagged and bound to the jealous custody of the rival interests of England until every fountain of wealth was hermetically sealed; and even the traditions of commercial enterprise had perished through desuetude."

During the reign of Charles II, England positively restricted Irish trade and commerce. The Irish were thoroughly skilled in wool work, long before the Flemish refugees began to teach it to the English workers. Irish woolen stuffs had a national reputation before manufactured cloth was introduced into England. In the 13th and 14th centuries, the Popes of Rome used to send their agents to several Irish towns to purchase woolen fabrics for the construction of their gorgeous mantles. On state occasions, Irish frieze was eagerly bought up in Spain and Italy, and so prized that garments made of it were entered in the "*wills*" of Florentine citizens as heirlooms. During the reigns of Edward III and Charles II, Irish cattle were permitted to be exported to England. The first navigation act of 1660 placed Ireland and England on equal terms regarding exports and imports, but the amended navigation act of 1663 failed to recognize Ireland.

All exportations from Ireland to English colonies, except victuals, servants, horses and salt, were prohibited; the act likewise forbade the exportation of Irish cattle to England. But this was not the worst, for three years later a similar embargo was put upon Irish beef, pork, bacon, butter and cheese. In 1634, Earl Stafford, the then Lord-lieutenant of Ireland, wrote to King Charles I: "That all wisdom advises to keep this kingdom of Ireland as much subordinate and dependant upon England as possible; and withholding them from the manufacture of wool, which, unless otherwise directed, I shall by all means discourage, and then enforcing them to fetch their clothing from thence and to take their salt from the King." This hint from Stafford appears to have directed England's future policy. For in 1673, forty years later, (Charles II's reign) Sir Wm. Temple, the Irish Viceroy, proposed that the manufacture of woolens should cease in Ireland. Athough this proposal had not an immediate effect, a bill was soon after passed in the English House of Commons, (1699) forbidding all exportation from Ireland to England or elsewhere of her woolen manufactures. This annihilated forthwith this staple industry, and opened one of the most painful epochs of Irish history. The linen trade, which at the time, was not in a very flourishing condition was also discouraged. Mr. Lecky states that Irish linen manufactures were excluded from England by the imposition of a duty of 30 per cent., whilst Ireland was not allowed to participate in the bounties granted for the exportation of the best description of linen shipped from Great Britain to foreign countries. England also strove to make Scotland outrival Ireland in her linen trade, by the granting a government subsidy to Scotch manufactures.

The cotton industry of Ireland was likewise discouraged by a duty of 25 per cent. A statute of George III made it a punishable offence to wear cotton fabrics unless they were made in Great Britain. The culture and capture of fish, the manufacture of glass, beer, malt —in fact, every lucrative industry poor Ireland* undertook to promote was immediately proscribed or dis-

* Generations after generations have been born with the words "poor Ireland" on their lips, and have died uttering the same suggestive syllables. It blusters and moans in every sough of the wind; it expands the sails of every ship that wanders over the ocean. The lordly trees that shiver before the emigrant's axe in primeval forests

couraged by the British government. Dean Swift was prosecuted by the government for publishing a pamphlet entitled "A proposal for the universal use of Irish manufactures."

fall a memento of poor Ireland." The engine that rattles over our trans-continental railroads, at every gust of smoke seems to belch them out. The words are raised into monumental stone and statue, as well in France, Spain, Austria—in the poet's corner of Westminster, under St. Patrick's, New York, as well as St. Patrick's, Dublin.—SAVAGE.

CHAPTER III.

WHAT IRELAND LOSES BY THE EXPORTATION OF CATTLE.

AT present, the exportation of cattle to England is not inhibited by the government—in fact, the English are the best markets for Irish cattle. Strange as it may appear, this is one of Ireland's greatest misfortunes, as the following argument, from the pen of a Limerick merchant (Mr. A. Shaw) clearly demonstrates. In reference to the exportation of sheep, he reasons thus:

"One pound in weight of wool is worth about 1s., and it may be roughly estimated as capable of producing one pound of a fairly good cloth. There are tweeds that go in price from 7s. to 8s. 6d. a yard wholesale, finer cloths from 14s. to 20s.; the red cloth for officers' uniforms costs a guinea a yard, and the scarlet fabric for a huntsman's coat 27s. a yard. Now, how is the pound of wool rendered so extremely valuable? By human labor! Leaving out of consideration those expensive kinds, let us take an ordinary common tweed at say 3s. per yard. One pound of wool making a yard of this cloth becomes tripled in value by labor. An average man requires about seven yards of cloth for a suit—this would be 21s. for the cloth—but, for argument's sake, suppose it costs

20s. There are 5,000,000 of people in Ireland, 2,000,000 of whom require (or should, if properly clad) two suits per annum, and so you have 4,000,000 suits in demand each year. These, at 20s. each, would cost £4,000,000, of which £2,666,666 is actual labor, and lost to us if the material is worked up elsewhere than in Ireland."

Ireland suffers a loss as great, if not greater, by the exportation of other cattle, such as cows, pigs, horses, poultry, game, etc.

Considering the long sea-passage from Irish ports to Liverpool or London, a great deterioration in value is caused thereby. It has been calculated that a beast shipped from Limerick or Galway to Liverpool entails a loss of thirty shillings; a summary of this annual loss to Ireland in the entire exportation of its cattle, would amount to one million pounds sterling ($5,000,000.)* This is a loss without gain to anybody. Now, we shall examine the losses entailed by the exportation of the raw material which support several remunerative industries in England: hides, that can be tanned into various grades of leather; horns, that can be converted into hafts of knives, buttons, combs, etc.; bones, into a thousand different uses; tallow, into soap and candles; hoofs, into jellies and jujubes; hair, into bristles and upholstery, and refuse, into glue. All these commodities are manufactured in England and sent back to Ireland at an advanced price. If we examine a respectable shopkeeper's premises or a farmer's homestead we shall find that almost every expensive article of furniture

---

* Mr. Tallerman, an English merchant, computes the waste by the exportation of live cattle from Ireland to England at £1,088,097 annually. (1889).

and farm implement has been made in England; cutlery, bearing a Sheffield, or some other English brand; china and crockery, that of Manchester, Bristol or Birmingham. In the latter city more than 35,000 families are employed in these manufactures; children from ten years of age, to old men and women of three score and ten are thus employed. How deplorable is the contrast in Ireland! In the largest cities, seldom more than one or two individuals of a household are employed; the rest of the family, however numerous, are obliged to remain idle. With the peasantry, this condition is even more aggravating. Should a farmer engage twelve members of his family cultivating his farm, at the end of the year, instead of being requited, he is frequently mulcted by the landlord who raises his rentals, thus confiscating the fruit of his labor.

But we have not yet exhausted the subject of English monopoly of materials that should be manufactured in Ireland. Last summer (1889) an American tourist challenged the proprietor of a large hotel in Dublin, to point out a single article of furniture in his house that was manufactured in Ireland. Chiffoniers, wardrobes, tables, bureaus, mirrors, lounges, sofas, piano, lace curtains, lambrequins, window-glass, mantels, vases, porcelain, china and glass-ware, chandeliers, table coverings, bedsteads, mattresses, carpets, brushes, toilet articles, pins, crayons and steel engravings—all these and a hundred other things were imported from England. In fact, almost all the traders and merchants of Ireland are supplied by England or America; tailors, shoe-makers, painters, blacksmiths, harness-makers, printers, milliners, etc. In the farm and farm-yard we see patent rakes, plows, sowing, reaping, mowing and threshing machines, shovels, pitchforks—in short, almost every implement a farmer needs, imported from England, America or the Continent.

Although the topography of various cities and towns of Ireland is more favorable to commerce and manufacture than most English or American cities, yet, while many of the latter are emporiums of manufacture and commerce, the former are totally ignored. What but manufactures support such cities--Manchester, with a population of 450,000; Birmingham, 400,000; Bristol, 250,000; Sheffield, 240,000; Leeds, 280,00; Hull, 135,000? The harbor of Galway or Queenstown is superior to that of Liverpool, yet these towns have a population of only eighteen and nine thousand, respectively, while Liverpool has more than 600,000 inhabitants. Hosiery and lace are the chief manufactures of Nottingham; woolen stockings and hosiery, of Leicester; silks, of Macclesfield and Coventry; crepes, of Norwich; pottery, of Newcastle; porcelain, of Worcester; carpets, of Kidderminster, and pins, of Gloucester. Could not all these industries exist in Ireland? Why must Ireland depend on England for the production of these goods when her own soil and people have similar, if not superior, advantages? A lack of sufficient capital and the ruthless monopoly of English trade, is the answer. If we look to this hemisphere, we find the same results. What would New England or, indeed, any of our great American cities be if manufactures were annihilated? Fall River, with a present population of 70,000, employs in its mills 40,000 operatives. These people would unquestionably starve were they to depend on the produce of agriculture or sale of cattle for subsistence. In fact, there is no arable land in the vicinage. Providence, with 125,000 inhabitants could scarcely subsist were all her factories, mills and foundries closed. Only a year ago Bristol, R. I., (6,000 inhabitants) was on the verge of bankruptcy when her rubber mill was closed; the failure of jewelry manufacture would paralyze every form of business in the flourishing towns of North and East Attleboro; Taunton, New Bedford, (Mass.,) Woonsocket, (R. I.,) with a majority of other New England cities depend on public works. It is even so with many of the greatest cities of the United States; agriculture contributes but a fraction of the support of New York, Philadelphia, Boston, Chicago, St. Louis, Cincinnati, New Orleans and Louisville.

Business is so still in Irish cities that the shutters of the leading and lesser business houses are seldom removed before half past eight or nine o'clock in the morning, whilst every store is expected to be closed by six o'clock in the evening, except apothecary and telegraph depots which, under no circumstances, transact business after eight o'clock, P. M. Every store and office is closed on Sundays.

CHAPTER IV.

FACTS AND FIGURES SHOWING THE DECADENCY OF SEVERAL CITIES AND TOWNS IN IRELAND.

A FEW years ago, the city of Cork was next to Dublin in population and commercial enterprise; at present, it has been superseded by Belfast with a population of 210,000 against that of Cork with a little more than 80,000 inhabitants. Thirty-five years ago, the population of Cork was almost double its present figures, while Belfast was but a village; at the same time, Limerick had a population of 70,000; to day, it has not more than 38,000. Immediately before and after the "Union" Galway had a population of 40,000; at present, it has not more than 18,000. Statistics show that the following cities within the past half century had more than double their present population: Waterford, 27,150; Kilkenny, 14,120; Wexford, 11,000; Ennis, 5,340. In England and America, towns of no greater size would be regarded as mere villages, unfit for postal delivery.

Dublin, the capital city of Ireland, at present is not much larger than Belfast, numbering only 249,602 inhabitants. The following description of the present condition of Dublin, by Mr. A. Shaw, will be found to be painfully interesting:

"In 1800, in Dublin alone, there were 15,000 silk weavers constantly employed—there are about 400 this moment. The woolen trade employed 23,000 hands at an average of 30 shillings a week; I can only recollect five or six such mills now, in and about Dublin, which might employ about 2,000 hands. The hat-making trade employed 850 hands; I don't believe there are 50 hat-makers in Dublin now. The hosiery trade employed 11,000. Is there any hosiery made in Dublin now? Ribbon weaving, 13,000 hands; men at 35 shillings a week, women at 14 shillings a week. Curriers, 200, at three pounds a week, and so on with other trades. If we have some other industries instead of these, it is no argument for general prosperity. The woolen industries had centres at Dublin, Cork, Limerick, Waterford, Bandon, Kilkenny, Carrick-on-Suir. Cotton industry—Dublin, Drogheda, Callan, Limerick, Bandon, etc. Hosiery—Belfast, Limerick, Lisburn, Waterford, Kilkenny, Carlow and Dundalk. Where are all these industries now? Alas! Echo answers—where? And in this connection I would ask: Where are the 98 Irish peers and a proportionate number of wealthy commoners who inhabited the city of Dublin prior to the Union, who kept their entire establishments there, and spent their rents where they could enrich the lands from which they were drawn, instead of filling the coffers of the already opulent London shopkeepers? The amount spent out of Ireland has been estimated at something like 4,000,000 pounds per annum. What country of the size of Ireland could have withstood this constant hemorrhage for over three quarters of a century without being bankrupt?"

In Mulhall's celebrated "Fifty Years of National Progress," (retrogression as far as Ireland is concerned) we find that Irish emigration since 1837 has amounted to almost 84 per cent. of the entire population. He tabulates it from 1837 to 1886; and for these forty-nine years shows that 4,186,000 people left Ireland, which is equal to 85,424 per year, or more than the present population of the city of Cork, twice that of Limerick and almost four times that of Waterford. It has been asserted that every able bodied emigrant to the United States is a net gain to the country of £200 ($1,000) per head. In one generation, 4,000,000 emigrants who left home penniless, have become possessed of real and personal property amounting to £665,000,000 sterling, besides having sent home to their friends a sum of £32,000,000. The two amounts added would almost pay the entire British national debt.* Mulhall avers that emigration robs Ireland of wealth amounting to £17,000,000 annually ($85,000,000). In opposition to those who insinuate that the Union has been beneficial to Ireland, we would ask in view of this alleged prosperity, how it happened that, in 1881, 600,000 persons were in receipt of Poor Law relief in Ireland? If the Union begat trade and commerce, how is it that, in that year, one in every nine of the population was a pauper? In the Nineteenth Century Magazine for March, 1889, Mr. Given, an indisputable authority, says: "The taxable income of Great Britain has increased enormously, and those of Ireland hardly at all. Ireland, in population, has sunk from one-third to one-seventh of Great Britain. Ireland's national debt in 1797, was under £4,000,000 sterling. Shortly after the Union, when her fiscal system was united with England's, (in 1815) Ireland's debt

---

* The national debt of Great Britain for 1888 was £700,000,000.

was £128,000,000, and in two years after (1817) it amounted to £150,000,000. In 1841 the taxation per head was 9s. 6.; in 1871 it was £1. 6s. 1d. Ireland, while constituting about one-twentieth of the United Kingdom in resources, nevertheless, pays almost one-tenth of the taxes, or more than twice as much as her proper share."

The Irish people have been deprived, not only of their lands, and that partition of commerce to which, as a part of the British Empire they are naturally entitled, but, owing to the stagnant condition of national and corporate enterprise, have also been bereaved of trades and professions which in foreign countries would materially aid them in their efforts to gain an independent livelihood. Hence, male and female emigrants from Ireland find themselves handicapped by German, Italian and French artisans. The greater portion of the class who emigrate from Ireland have no knowledge of the mechanism of spinning, weaving, dyeing, printing, paper-making, etc.

It is passing strange, and a culpable oversight on the part of many Irish parents, that their children should be innocent of the more common and useful trades that require less skill, such as carpentry, blacksmithing, masonry, painting, shoe-making, tailoring, etc. It is true the laboring populace have but sorry opportunities of learning telegraphy, telephony, music, type-writing, type-setting, etc.; but the ordinary trades might be acquired by the men, whilst the young women might become expert at home in various industries, such as plain and fancy sewing, embroidery, millinery, dress-making, etc. A majority of Irish emigrants are only fit for farming—a business which they seldom or never follow in this country. Although many of them are well educated in didactic branches, they are incapable of adapting them to the American system. Book-keeping, surveying, school-teaching and a thousand other professions have domestic features and facilities that are quite unknown in Europe. Although physically and mentally capable, yet for at least six months after landing an Irish emigrant is unfit to discharge the duties of clerk in a dry goods, grocery or apothecary store, or in any American patent agency. Besides, emigrants need not expect to compete with native Americans in any of those offices that are the gift of the city or government. The latter have, what poor emigrants cannot expect to have, personal and political influence, and local acquaintance with merchants and mercantile business. Hence, a majority of the Irishmen who come to this country are obliged to seek employment as porters, teamsters, railway and street laborers, etc., whilst the Irish girls seek employment in hotels, boarding houses and private families, considering themselves lucky if their services are secured in such places. Indeed, there is much truth in the aspersion that the Irish emigrants are only fit to be ' *hewers*" of wood and "*drawers*" of water.

In the foregoing allegations I did not mean to insinuate that Irish emigrants are physically or intellectually deficient. On the contrary, I do not hesitate to aver that no people, with the few opportunities they have had in their native country, have made greater progress, or become more useful citizens. Many Irishmen who left their homes some thirty or forty years ago are to-day occupying some of the highest positions in our cities and government.

#

OTHER IRISH GRIEVANCES—DEGENERACY OF FISHERIES AND WOOD INDUSTRY, Etc.

TO all strangers and tourists who visit Ireland, it appears an insolvable question why such an inexhaustible source of wealth as the fishing industry should be almost entirely neglected. The question becomes more perplexing when we consider that Ireland has a coast line of 250 miles, indented with some of the finest fishing harbors in the word. Various reasons have been assigned for this apparently culpable neglect. Some writers attribute it to the Celtic origin of the inhabitants, insinuating that such a people lack sufficient patience for such a monotonous enterprise; yet the Cornishmen, Manxmen and Argylemen, the best fishermen in the United Kingdom, are of Celtic origin. The fishermen of St. Piérre and Miquelon, two islands in the St. Lawrence, and the colony of Cloddagh, near Boston, U. S., (an offshoot of Cloddagh in Co. Galway) brave the Atlantic waves in their canoes or carraghs of hoops and tarred canvas. Fishing was once a most flourishing industry in Ireland. Early in the 17th century, Wexford alone exported 100,000 barrels of herrings per annum. In the same century, Irish fishing waters were regarded so valuable that the Dutch paid Charles I £30,000 for the privilege of fishing in the western coast; Philip II, of Spain, paid £1,000 a year for the privilege of fishing in the northern coast. Immediately after the Union, Irish sea-fishing began to decline, owing to the sinister interference of the British government. The government paid £21,000 to encourage the importation into Ireland of British and colonial cured fish, and but £4,000 to encourage the exportation of Irish cured fish. Here then is a clear odds of five to one against Ireland. From 1829 to 1844, Scotland received a government grant of £200,000 ($1,000,000) for her fisheries, while Ireland only received £13,000. Irish merchants applied for a government brand such as Scotland secured, but were refused by a large majority of the House of Commons, consisting chiefly of English and Scotchmen. "It is a standing reproach to the British government," says a modern statesman, "to allow those fishing industries to remain undeveloped." In the United States, some 30,000 skilled naturalists are employed, furnished with a complete marine laboratory, several fish-hatching establishments, and a large steamer costing over $300,000, for the purpose of making observations around the coasts. In less than two years, America has expended for the development of this industry, not less than $200,000. If England were to contribute to pisciculture a tithe of what she expends on such luxuries as war ships and iron clads, she would have the lasting gratitude of the Irish people. It is shameful negligence on the part of the government that at present there does not exist a single chart of the deep sea fisheries of Ireland. Sea fishing would not only furnish employment to thousands who would follow this avocation, but would open another lucrative employment for men and women, such as boat building, sail and rope making, the weaving of nets and other piscatory utensils that at present are made in Penzance, the Isle of Man, and other English ports. A fishing school has been recently established at Baltimore, Co. Cork, which from the patronage extended to it by Irish Bishops,* promises to be successful. In the list of Irish grievances we would also include the almost total neglect of oyster culture, a most lucrative industry if properly cultivated.

† REAFFORESTATION AND WOOD INDUSTRY.

At one time there were numerous forests in Ireland, which contributed to render the climate genial and healthful. The wood was used in various industries; it was mainly used in the manufacture of farm implements and household furniture, smelting of iron, etc. This destruction has continued for ages, whilst replanting has been entirely neglected. It has been calculated that

* The Baroness Burdette-Coutts has made munificent gifts of money towards this industry in Baltimore.

† In Nebraska (America) fifteen years ago a voluntary movement was started for the encouragement of planting and reafforesting in general, and one day in the year, called "Arbor day," set apart for the purpose. On that occasion trees are planted by prominent persons and by the local bodies. This example has been followed by several other Western States, and "Arbor day" is now a public holiday in those regions, the date being fixed by the governor of the state. So great has been the growth, that in Kansas alone there are now no less than 250,000 acres of artificial forest, and *forty-three million forest trees* are growing in Nebraska, where two years ago not a single tree could be seen growing upon the wide prairies.

NOTE. The Dublin Freeman, of Jan., 1890, announces the ruthless sale (for the manufacture of matches) of the beautiful forests surrounding "the sweet vale of Aroca," Co. Wicklow.

the forests have been denuded at the rate of a thousand acres a year. The result is that the country is gradually losing its most useful and lucrative industry. Besides the shelter trees afford to man and beast, they frequently prevent inundation, and moderate the violence of winds and storms. In nature, there is no material more indispensable and valuable than wood. Human labor can convert it into a thousand articles of daily use. In Germany, there are entire districts wholly dependent for their living on the forests and contingent wood industries, while thousands live by wood carving in Switzerland. The whole district of Sonnenberg, on the borders of the Thuringian forests, gives employment to 43,000 hands, engaged in the craft of making dolls and other juvenile toys. This enterprise yields an annual income of $5,000,000, employing children as well as men and women of every age.

Rodach, another little German town in a mountainous district employs thousands of male and female hands making wicker baskets, glass marbles, imitation pearl beads, glass eyes, etc. They are enabled to do this by the presence of kasline and soda in the soil, otherwise so sterile that it is incapable of producing potatoes, except in patches. Nuremberg, by similar employment, yields $125,000 a year. Other sources of wealth, such as fruit growing, slate and marble quarrying, are industries that could be made most remunerative, but at present are sadly neglected. No slate imported from Scotland or England can compare with that of Killaloe and other Irish quarries in quality and durability, while the specimens of marble are the finest that can be produced in the United Kingdom.

IRISH BANK SYSTEM,* RAILWAY RATES, AND DECAY OF CELTIC ART.

The following sketch from the pen of a distingnished Irish financier, is entitled to particular notice:

"Moneys invested in stocks, bank and post-office deposits and other money saving institutions are computed at $4,000,000. Five-sixths of this capital is invested by the banker in all sorts of foreign bonds: for instance, in Suez canal bonds or railroads in Nicaragua; water-works in Juan Fernandez, anywhere and everywhere except in the country that created it. They will trust anybody before an Irishman.

When the Irish banks lend money, it is only a three month's bill at an enormous interest and with crippling security. A report of the sub-commission on the subject, in 1885, shows that the interest of the Irish public in the nine Irish banks is nearly four times that of the share holders, and declares, without reservation, that the banking laws of Ireland are *penal laws* of the worst kind.

If a small manufacturer, with machinery, plant and building costing £2,000, ($10,000) goes to a bank in the south or west of Ireland, for an advance to carry on or extend his business, he must pledge his entire property as collateral, besides his own, and often a friend's personal security; he may possibly then get from the bank a promissory note for £500, discounted for three months at six per cent.; or, in plainer words, he receives £200 for £2,000 of real outlay, and two men's personal security. We must here bear in mind that this £500 so

---

* There are nine different bank corporations which have branches in all the important towns of Ireland.

grudgingly lent him at this high rate of interest, is not a part of the bank shareholders' immediate capital, but possibly the deposits of the very borrower's own sisters, cousins, aunts and uncles, living, perhaps, in his own neighborhood, and receiving but one or one and a half per cent."

The following, on railway rates, is from the same writer:

RAILWAY RATES.

"Manufactured goods from Manchester to Tralee are charged 57s. 6d. per ton freight; from Manchester to Cork, 42s. 6d.; therefore, 15s. per ton divides the two places. But if a Cork manufacturer sends his goods from Cork to Tralee, the "local rate," as it is termed, is 36s. 3d., or 21s. 3d. more than the Manchester man pays. Again, woolen goods from Bradford to Tralee cost 77s. 6d. per ton, while the same class of goods sent from Cork to Tralee direct cost 58s., leaving only 19s. 6d. per ton carriage Bradford to Cork. It is, as a matter of fact, cheaper to get goods from an English manufacturing town in Yorkshire than from Dublin to Galway, or *vice versa.* Goods of ordinary class from Limerick to Belfast, via Dublin, cost 40s. a ton, while you can send the same goods to London for 25s. a ton. It is cheaper to send goods to Belfast *thus* than to rail them via Dublin—Limerick to Waterford by rail, steamer to Glasgow, then steamer to Belfast. From Limerick to Londonderry or Coleraine would be about as feasible as sending to Japan, through excessive railway rates. The freights upon Irish railways* seem to be arranged so as to dis-

---

* There are but nineteen broad-gauge railways in Ireland.

courage to the utmost our local developments, and encourage importation of all foreign goods from England and abroad."

A person accustomed to American railway travel would consider the Irish and, indeed, all European railway carriages barbarous vehicles, improvised for rough transportation rather than for commodious and comfortable locomotion. Whilst palace, dining and sleeping carriages are unknown in Ireland, and only employed in two or three railroads in England and Scotland, the meaningless and rude system of locking railway compartments (each capable of holding not more than ten persons) and the failure to furnish them with heating and other sanitary furniture, renders travelling, if not a risky, an arduous undertaking. The shortness of travelers' local destination is the only ostensible excuse for this lack of humane precaution. But it seems cruel, if not outrageous, to test by mileage, a traveler's physical endurance of cold, thirst, and common decency. The integrity and morality of the Irish people alone prevent the commission of dreadful crimes during railway travel.

DECAY OF CELTIC ART.

The reader, comparing the past flourishing condition of Celtic art with its present forlorn degeneracy, will find the following epitomized reference to ancient Celtic art a sad commentary. Celtic art held a place distinctively apart from that of other races, although the influence of Roman models was felt in the architecture, literature, painting and sculpture of the whole Western Europe. Ireland, however, adhered to her own ideals, and throughout the 700 years of her existence as an independent christian country, produced more and better art work than any other nation of the known world.

While nothing has been left undone to preserve the antiquities of Great Britain, the collection in the English Museum is far inferior to the Irish.

In gold and bronze ornaments and in illuminated manuscripts the Celt has left the Anglo-Saxon far behind. The same can be said in the matter of building supremacy. Only 20 structures of Anglo-Saxon times are standing, while several hundred edifices erected by the Celts prior to the 12th century show their superiority as architects.

Many of the finest exhibits in the English Museum are of Irish origin. For instance, the "Book of Lindisfarne," one of the finest illuminated manuscripts in the world, is the work of Irish monks who settled in Northern Ireland 1,200 years ago.

Irish art has been traced back to a time beyond a written history of the island itself. Buried urns, dug up from time to time, show that decorative art was known before the introduction of christianity upon the island, the urns being of the most exquisite designs.

The bronze tools and weapons, which are found in abundance, and which were certainly made at least 1,900 years ago, show that Celtic art had attained a certain degree of perfection even in that far day.

The collection of bells, chimes, crosses and other ecclesiastical objects in the museum of the Royal Irish Academy, is perhaps the finest in the world, and takes the art student back into Pagan times, 1,400 years ago.

Gold seems to have been the favorite decorative metal of Ireland; and judging by the quantities of golden relics that have been found in Ireland, there must have been vast stores of it there in "the brave days of old."

The masterpieces of ancient Irish art, however, are the golden reliquaries, chalices, Celtic and other crosses, and several smaller articles.

Cases for the preservation of books are classified with the finest samples of the Irish art. The most celebrated of these is a case made for preserving the copy of the Gospels known as the "Domnach Airgid," which is said to have been brought to Ireland by St. Patrick himself. The book is of the highest antiquity. It was originally placed in a wooden box, which in the 12th century was cased in a copper and silver shrine of rich device, and in the 14th century the latter was itself inclosed in a casket of silver and gold.

Celtic sculpture is as peculiar and superior as its other forms of art, and bears the same stamp of laborious finish; but it does not seem that statuary was ever much practiced in ancient Ireland, save in connection with the detached monuments erected to record public events or honor the mighty dead. The crosses, covered with relief pictures, in stone, are still numerous in Ireland, and constitute as typical a class of its antiquities as the round towers which lend so romantic a touch to its scenery.

The celebrated cross at Clonmacnoise, erected as a memorial of the monarch, Flan, in the year 912, is "a thing of beauty," but is far surpassed by that at Tuam, erected in 1123. The latter was originally 30 feet high, but has been lowered by breaking on the part of vandals.

The "Book of Kells," which is now in the library of Trinity College, Dublin, is a splendid MS. copy of the four Gospels, written on parchment, in Latin, and richly ornamented with illuminations. It dates from the 8th century, and was then produced by the monks of the monastery of Kells. Each gospel is prefaced by an illuminated page, having reference to the manuscript following, and containing both figures and scrolls of the most varied and beautiful designs, coupled with a brilliancy of coloring which is simply marvelous, when the age of the volume and the vicissitudes it has undergone are taken into consideration. Not alone the title page, but the capital letters, are in scroll form and richly colored, and the Celtic designs are of such beauty that they are now reproduced in every description of art needle-work. The "Book of Kells" was jealously guarded from its earliest years, and tradition affirms that it was kept in a case of gold and finally stolen from the monastery for sake of its golden cover. Subsequently it came into the hands of Ussher, Archbishop of Armagh, and was by him presented to Trinity College, together with other valuable works, about the year 1856.

CHAPTER VI.

LANDLORDISM AND THE LAND QUESTION.

ALTHOUGH, in the foregoing pages, we have exposed many obstacles that militate against the social and national prosperity of Ireland, we have not yet related the chief source of Ireland's depression and discontent. The heading of the above chapter may be regarded as the mainspring of the nation's positive grievances and its past and present agitations.*

Landlordism did not originate with the alleged "Union" of Great Britain and Ireland (1800-1801). It took its rise during the reign of Queen Elizabeth, in the beginning of the 17th century. While landlordism in other countries is a tolerable, and frequently a laudable institution, in Ireland it is considered a synonym for unmitigated oppression and confiscation. In our discussion of this subject we would respectfully submit that we have no penchant for using strong language or unguarded assertions in our reference to the British government. We shall, as far as possible, confine our remarks to historical or incontestable facts. Although Elizabeth left no lawful issue to inherit the English

---

* Fully five-sixths of the population depend on agriculture for subsistence.

throne, and has been styled by her admirers "The VIRGIN QUEEN," the fact that she conceived and brought forth this monstrous offspring "*Landlordism*," hale and hardy, cannot be contested. Prolonging this metaphor, we would aver it was an abortion, baptized in bigotry, and supported from this Queen's time to the present, by rigorous and ruthless oppression. In those days, however, the features of landlordism were different from its present aspect. It was the pretence of religion, and not the mere desire of sordid gain that induced Elizabeth to institute and maintain landlordism, or what was practically the same, to sanction the confiscation of Catholic property. Had Ireland, like England and Scotland, renounced Catholicism, she would then, and to-day, be prosperous and free. King Henry VIII, Elizabeth's reputed father, merely confiscated churches and monasteries in his bold efforts to exterminate Catholicity; but Elizabeth, under the pretext of promoting Protestantism, seized 870,000 acres of Irish land—six entire counties, known at present as the Black North or Ulster reservation.

After Elizabeth's death, in 1650, Oliver Cromwell, who succeeded her in power, but not in heredity, (after the execution of King Charles I) seized 3,000,000 acres. In the fever of his wrath, he took active steps to drive every Irish man, woman and child out of the soil. In executing this scheme, he arrogated infernal as well as political authority, by commanding his soldiery to drive the Irish either to hell or to Connaught.* A majority of the peasantry preferred to go to Connaught, naturally

* Parts of Connaught were then so barren that it was said they did not contain wood enough to burn, water enough to drown, or earth enough to bury a man.

concluding the other climate would be reserved for Cromwell and his friends. Indeed, to the present day the *"curse of Cromwell"* is regarded a most appalling malediction amongst the people, who, on the mention of his name, mark their foreheads with the sign of the cross. Wherever the *"shades"* of Cromwell have been detained since he lived in the flesh, it is certain his evil genius, while promoting the cause of landlordism, wrought untold misery on Ireland and the Irish people.

In 1691, during the reign of King William of Orange, Ireland was so completely confiscated that there was not, throughout the entire length and breadth of the land, a single Catholic land owner. The farmers were reduced to a wretched state of tenantry, not better, if equal to the condition of the negro in slavery times. Hence, Orangemen and the landed gentry of Ireland have good reason to hail the memory of King William, and the anniversary of the battle of the Boyne on the 12th of every July, the day which commemorates Ireland's defeated efforts to regain national independence. Ever since King William landed in Ireland, down to the present year, every picture of Ireland represents a series of cruel evictions and national oppression.

For the year 1881, there were 17,641 evictions in various parts of the country; during the year 1889,* no less than 500 evictions have taken place on the Olphert and Clanricarde estates alone. Many of these evictions (according to Mr. Gladstone) are equivalent to so many sentences of death. A contributor to the Contemporary Review, (Dec. 1888) wrote as follows:—"Practically the same dreadful quarrel remains; it is still for the peasant

---

* Total number of evictions for 1889 amounted to 4,000.

as it has been for centuries, the struggle about arrears, about a burden of indebtedness which the tenant cannot shake off, and which it is impossible for him to pay, and which ever keeps him at the mercy of his landlord. The poor tenants pay the so-called rent, not out of the produce of the soil, for that barely suffices them to exist, but out of their earnings elsewhere. Rent, in such a case, (and this is true of the enormous proportion of Irish tenants) is mere plunder and blackmail, wrung out of the necessities of starving men for the right to live. . . . Practically, the struggle between poor and rich in Ireland, between Catholic and Protestant, between Irishmen and Englishmen, is the same to-day that it has been for more than a century, mitigated in part, with several of its enormities removed, most of the bigotry and blood thirstiness extinct, but with the most systematic apparatus of martial law applied to a European people, in the absence of war, and with the original and even fundamental enormity increased in force, viz: that millions upon millions of the earnings of half-starved Irish laborers are sent over yearly to mere foreign creditors, whose very names are hardly known, and who never spent one sixpence on tenants, land, or Ireland, and who have no moral right whatever to receive back a sixpence, except so far as it appears in a series of documents all based upon confiscation."

Mr. Lefevre, M. P., in his book, "Two Centuries of Irish History," says:—(Oct., 1888) "A whole township has been cleared of its tenants; twenty-three families have been evicted from their homes, and many of these and their friends, forty in number, have been committed to prison for resisting these evictions. The tenants have lost all their rights under the last act of 1881."

. . . . "We find another estate with 4,500 tenants. Their rent is wholly paid out of earnings which they make at a distance. There, for eighty years, the landlords have never resided, but have drawn their large rentals and spent them in England. No capital has ever been expended by them in improving the property. Every improvement which has brought the land into cultivation from its original condition of waste bog has been effected by the tenants; all the houses and buildings have been erected by them. And yet the rentals have been increased from £5,000 to £24,000 within a century. During the 17th and 18th centuries, the persecution of Catholics, and the spoliation or confiscation of their property were means employed to extirpate Catholicity. Blind zeal and bigotry were the chief motives for the oppression of Irishmen before the 'Union,' ever since, avarice has played an active, if not a chief part."

An eminent French historian, (De Beaumont) visiting Ireland in 1824, declared: That he had seen the Indian in his wigwam, and the Negro in his chains, but that the condition of the Irish peasant was beneath that of the slave or savage. It must be admitted that there have been some just and humane landlords who consulted the interests and happiness of their tenantry, but they were a forlorn minority. A majority of the landed gentry had grown accustomed to regard the whole produce of the land as their natural right. The following extract from the letter of a landlord to his agent (1889) bears out this assertion: "I may tell you that I would not now accept 99 per cent. of the rent and costs due to me, as I am going to clear Dringlass and Glasacoo. Remember they (the tenants) are merely living on *my* *land* as long as I let them, and will not regard costs in carrying out my plans. I intend that in five, or at most, in ten years, there will not be a family living there."* Such men as Clanricarde, Olphert, the O'Grady, O'Callahan, Ponsonby, Smith-Barry and Lord Londonderry are living embodiments of those human monsters whom the mild Berkeley called *"vultures with iron bowels."* Nowhere in Europe was there a propertied class who did so little for, and took away so much from the people. Impossible rent was kept in the books of an estate, and arrears recorded to hold the tenant in perpetual bondage. A farmer might improve his land by building, draining, fertilizing, etc. Instead of recompensing, the landlord invariably raised the rent in proportion to the tenant's improvements. It made no difference whether the farmer, with his family of eight or ten children, had labored for years upon the land. The farmer received no recompense for his own and his family's industry, even in cases where the soil, entirely barren when first occupied, was rendered fertile by the tenant's labor and outlay. In numerous instances tenants were not allowed to hunt, fish or cut turbary in their own farms, whilst under no circumstances could they divide or sell their interest in them. Things must have come to a sad pass in Ireland when such a bigot as Jas. Anthony Froude once declared, "That if a legion of angels inhabited Ireland, they would lose their temper, if treated as Irishmen have been."

Rent, in other countries, meant a surplus after the farmer had been duly paid for his labor; in Ireland, it

---

* The London Times once exultingly predicted that a Celtic Irishman would be as scarce in Connemara as a red Indian on the shores of Manhattan.

meant the whole produce of the soil, except the potato pit. If the farmer strove for more, his master knew how to bring him to submission; he could carry away his implements of trade; he could, and frequently did, seize the stools and pots in his miserable cabin, the planks that sheltered his children, and the cow that yielded them nourishment.

CHAPTER VII.

IRISH FAMINES AND EVICTIONS.

THE great famines of 1812, '22 and '46 were not natural but artificial. It was only the potato that rotted; there was abundance of other produce in the country if the people had only consumed it. John Mitchell, in his book "Prison Life," states that during the famine of '46, 1,200,000 persons (more than 300,000 families) perished. During this dreadful time, Ireland was annually exporting to England, food valued at £14,000,000 sterling. From the port of Newry, during the rage of the famine, eleven ships sailed for England, laden with provisions, besides two steamers which sailed four times a week; one of these steamers contained 4,000 barrels of wheat, 11,000 quarters of oats and 7,700 firkins of butter. The government returns of 1849 show that Ireland paid altogether in taxes to the British exchequer no less a sum than £13,293,681, while her starving people exported to England 595,000 head of cattle, 840,000 sheep, 959,000 quarters of wheat, 700,000 swine, 3,600,000 quarters of oats and meal. The population was only 8,000,000, and the soil of Ireland, according to Sir Robert Kane, in his "Industrial Resources," is capable of supporting 20,000,000 people. While the Ameri-

cans, and even the negroes were sending money to the
famine sufferers in Ireland, England, her so-called sister
kingdom, demanded her seasoned or bloody pound of
flesh. Writing of his visit to Ireland during the lesser
famine of 1880, Mr. James Redpath states that thousands would have perished if it were not for the munifi-
cence of the American and Australian Irish and the contributions of the New York Herald and the Duchess of
Marlborough. The Prince of Wales lent his name, but
little of the royal purse towards the Mansion House
Relief Committee. "The facts of Irish destitution,"
says the London Times, "are ridiculously simple; the
people never suffer from a natural, but from an artificial
famine. Nature has done well for Ireland. The land
is full and overflowing with human food. But something ever interposes between the hungry mouth and
the ample banquet. The famished victim of a mysteri-
ous sentence stretches out his hands to the viands which
his own industry has placed before his eyes, but no
sooner are they touched than they disappear. A perpetual decree of *sic vos, non vobis*, condemns him to toil
without enjoyment." Referring to the extraordinary
exodus of the Irish, another writer says:

"The tales of horror from Ireland of tens of thousands of people dying of starvation within five hours'
sail of English shores, within sixty miles of the wealth-
iest country in the world, by which the people of Ireland
were ruled, ship loads of dying and fever-stricken emigrants arriving in the Atlantic ports, adding sights of
suffering to tales of starvation. From the shores of the
Atlantic to the banks of the Mississippi, the path of the
fleeing Irish exiles was one long string of graves. In

the thirty-seven years the emigrants from the six counties of Munster have numbered 1,117,921, or 73.3 per cent. of the average population. Assuredly, it is a sorrowful record Dr. Stratten writes about, about this shipment of human beings: 'Up to November, one emigrant in every seven had died, and during November and December there have been many deaths in the different emigrant hospitals, so that it is understating the mortality to say that one person in every five was dead by the end of the year.'

"The evicted tenants who were landed in New York fared even more horribly. They were transported across the Atlantic in what have been only too truly described as 'the coffin ships,' which were freighted with the victims of landlordism and misrule. The Erin Queen sailed with 493 passengers, of whom 136 died on the voyage amidst scenes which could hardly have been surpassed in the crowded and sickly slavers on the African coast. It appears, writes Dr. Stratten in the 'Edinburgh Medical Journal,' that out of 552 passengers who sailed in the Avon, 246 died, and amongst 476 on board another ship, the Virginius, not less than 267 deaths took place. Of 440 on the Larch, 108 died, and 150 were seriously diseased. The Chief Secretary for Ireland reported with regard to the 89,783 persons who embarked for Canada in 1847, that 6,100 perished on the voyage, 4,100 on their arrival, 5,200 in hospitals, 1,900 in towns to which they repaired. How some of these unhappy cargoes of humanity were made up has been explained by an English gentleman employed as conducting engineer of Public Works in Ireland during the famine, Mr. William Henry Smith, C. E., who, referring to the part of Connaught in which he was stationed at the time, writes thus: 'Hundreds, it is said, had been compelled to emigrate by ill usage (on the part of the landlords), and in one vessel, containing 600, not one hundred survived. From Grosse Island, the great charnel house of victimized humanity, up to Port Sarnia, and along the borders of our magnificent river, upon the shores of Lakes Ontario and Erie, wherever the tide of emigration has extended, are to be found the final resting places of the sons and daughters of Erin, one unbroken chain of graves, where repose fathers and mothers, sisters and brothers, in one co-mingled heap, without a tear bedewing the soil, or a stone marking the spot where their bones repose.'

" Now, as heretofore, they are the young and vigorous who seek shelter beyond the seas from the miseries that misrule creates. Last year more than 80 per cent. of the emigrants were between the ages of 15 and 35; and that headlong rush is from a country where every year thousands of acres are relapsing into moorland and marsh for want of hands to till it--or, we should say, by reason of laws that shut out the soil from the labour that would save it from waste."

EVICTIONS.

As there is no more endearing place in creation than home, especially the ancestral home, where kindred generations have lived and died, there can be no sentence, except that of death, more painful than that which consigns an individual or family to banishment from their native hearth. The reader, therefore, will find the following brief sketch of evictions that include, not only the razing and ruin of homes, but the confiscation of present and past industry, painfully interesting. The annual list of evictions establishes an appalling proof of oppression and property. Imagine 17,641 evictions in one year! Savage as well as civilized nature revolts against the destruction of so many homesteads. The hostile bias of the government is not less culpable, we should say *criminal*, than the obduracy of the landlords. Frequently, regiments of constablery and soldiery, consisting of two hundred, and sometimes five hundred men, with a platoon of bailiffs and unprincipled emergency men and a battering-ram, invade a poor Irishman's peaceful dwelling. The duty of this mighty army of dissolute military is not discharged until they see cast on the roadside, a helpless family, of different ages, from the suckling babe to the bed-ridden grandmother.

The peasantry usually resist, being loath to leave the roof-tree of their ancestors, however humble.* The defensive course which some tenants adopt is ludicrous in the face of an army of government officials. The *boreen*, or bye-road, leading to the doomed homestead, is obstructed by felled trees or impassable rocks; the windows and doors are also barricaded with gnarled logs or thorn brush. Hot water, pitch or lime wash is sometimes dispensed from the roof or windows. Now and then the smiling face of some young girl or the scowling visage of an old woman nestled in white cap and borders, is seen to emerge from the ordinary or improvised apertures, and simultaneously the fragments of some culinary or chamber missiles are directed towards the heads and shoulders of the bailiffs or emergency men. In five

---

* Even animals of the brute creation obstinately cling to their habitations.

instances, (1889) three young women "held the fort," and in one instance, a girl of fifteen defended her father's house for two hours against the united forces of military and bailiffs. But the final seizure of the homestead and surrender of its occupants might easily be anticipated. Although wielded by more vigorous hands, a blackthorn stick or piece of delf is no efficient weapon against a bayonet, a sword, or a musket. During most evictions, the delf and furniture of the poor tenants are rudely cast into the streets or rendered unfit for future use; whilst, in many instances, the young girls of the evicted household are insulted by half drunken bailiffs, emergency men or soldiers. Two soldiers were last year indicted in Luggacurran for having defloured a young girl after she had been evicted from her home.

This is not the end of this shameful farce. Before the poor family are permitted to enter the Poor House or emigrant ship, the elder members who resisted are imprisoned for a period, ranging from six weeks to six months. Innocent little boys and girls too, have been often punished in this fashion. The accused are seldom tried in their own barony or district, lest they should have sympathizing friends among the jury; their venue is generally transferred to Belfast, Maryborough or some other district where Orangeism prevails. The patriot Archbishop Croke of Cashel, in his letter to the Bishop of Raphoe, (Jan. 12, '89) stated: "As far as I know, and I know a good deal about savage, as well as civilized countries, there is no land on the face of the habitable globe, except unhappy Ireland, in which such scandalous, heartrending, and unchristian scenes could take place with any approach to impunity, or without much fierce contention and even blood-shed. Sending the armed forces of the Crown to tear down the roof-trees and demolish the humble dwellings of the poor for the benefit of a pampered few, appears to me to be a sin that cries to Heaven for vengeance; and surely, if Holy Writ has consigned to everlasting perdition the heartless creatures who refuse shelter to those that need it, what must be thought of our present moralizing rulers who, far from being content with the negative attitude of non-intervention, bring all the weight of their authority to sanction such guilty excesses, and hold in hand a gang of ruthless desperadoes to execute their nefarious purposes."*

The following harrowing account of evictions appeared in the Dublin Weekly Freeman, Nov., 1889:

"There is no other civilized or half civilized country in which the savageries of the last week's eviction campaign in the desolate region of Falcarragh would be patiently endured. The man that would emulate in England the atrocities of Olphert in Ireland would be universally shunned and execrated as a monster. The

---

* Von Raumer, making a tour in Ireland, tries to explain to his own country people the state of things produced by the landlord land-laws of this country thus:—"How shall I translate *tenant-at-will?* Shall I say *serfs?* No; in feudal times serfdom consisted rather in keeping the vassals attached to the soil, and by no means in driving them away. An ancient vassal is a lord compared with the present tenant-at-will, to whom the law affords no defence. Why not call them *Wegjagdbare* (chaseable)? But this difference lessens the analogy—that for hares, stags, and deer, there is a season during which no one is allowed to hunt them, whereas tenants-at-will are hunted all the year round. And if anyone would defend his farm (as badgers and foxes are allowed to defend their cover), it is here denominated 'rebellion!'"

government that dared abet him in his work of wanton cruelty would be driven from power by a storm of indignation. The Septennial Act would not save them a day from the fierce wrath of the people. Can anyone fancy for a moment a force of one hundred and fifty English soldiers, armed to the teeth, deputed by the government to guard a gang of ruffians in their work of wrecking and burning an English hamlet and savagely maltreating the inhabitants? In England the idea is too startling to be entertained; in Ireland the reality is too common to be wondered at.

"The scenes that disgraced last week's man-hunting in the wilds of Falcarragh are so startling as to be almost incredible. At the house of a man named Devir, the chief huntsman, Hewson, and his bloodhounds kept howling that the wretched tenant who lay helpless on a sick bed should be thrown out on the roadside. They drew off at last, muttering and growling, only when the medical certificate of the army doctor declared that the eviction would mean murder. When the humble homestead of the poor Widow Cole was burst into by those devils in human form—the emergency men—the shrieks of women in agony, heard beyond the wide cordon of soldiers drawn round the building to preserve the sacred privacy of eviction, announced to the breathless spectators that some exceptional savagery was in progress. A few moments later a soldier sneaked down, in a shamefaced way, for lint and plaster, and medical appliances.

"'Then the wounded girl, Bridget Conaghan,' (we quote *verbatim* the description of an eye witness), 'was dragged out with her head split open with the blow of a crowbar, wielded by one of the emergency men! The poor girl was helped down the lane by two policemen with the blood streaming from a big gash just above the right ear. The whole side of the face, neck and shoulder were covered with blood. She and her three companions were placed under arrest, though the emergency man whom she identified as her assailant was allowed to go about his business.'

CHILD TORTURERS.

"Such is the merciful and impartial administration of the law in Falcarragh. Scarcely less piteous was the scene at the house of the tenant, Magee, whose twin infant children were dragged from their bed by the emergency men and carelessly thrown half naked on the bare earth in the biting air of October, their little limbs blue with the cold, and their piteous wailing almost frozen on their lips, while their weeping mother was mercilessly hustled away from their side outside the wide cordon of police and soldiery.

"More inhuman still and more revolting, if that be possible, was the following incident vividly described by the special correspondent of the Freeman on the spot:

"'A rather long tramp brought us to the house of Manus M'Ginley, a little 'shieling' on the roadside. The house was occupied by the tenant, and his father and mother. He only returned from jail on Saturday last, and now on Thursday he again had the bitter experience of an eviction. His wife, the tenant's mother, has been an invalid for seventeen years. To-day the emergency men pitched her out on the street without a moment's hesitation. The poor old creature became so ill on being evicted that she seemed in danger of death.

Father Boyle, who was present, deemed it necessary to administer the last sacraments, and a soldier was despatched in hot haste for Dr. M'Laughlin. The doctor on arriving said the woman should not have been removed, as her life was in serious danger. He spoke to Mr. Cameron, and suggested the necessity of having her put into bed in her son's house again, as there was no bed in the little cabin to which she was carried. To this humane suggestion the Divisional Commissioner replied that he would try and get her into the workhouse, which, be it remembered, is ten miles away. A very heartless feature of the case was the refusal of permission to the old woman's husband to go to her assistance. A kind hearted policeman allowed him to pass the cordon, but by order of District-Inspector Hill he was immediately put back again, and would not be allowed to approach his invalid wife who was lying in a fainting condition on the bare stones of the street within ten yards of him.'

"In the sheer wantonness of triumphant cruelty—such cruelty as a savage might glory in—the emergency men, by order of their masters, poured libations of petroleum on the ruined homes of the evicted tenants, which their own hands had built, and burned them to the ground as an acceptable holocaust to the twin divinities of 'Law and Order' in Ireland. Even on evidence the most conclusive, it is hard to believe that such things are possible in a civilized land—possible to be done, possible to be borne."

Heart-rending evictions of similar character have taken place during the past two years, under the immediate supervision of Her Majesty's police and military, on the Clongorey, Luggacurran, Gweedore, Olphert, Ponsonby, Smith-Barry, Delmage and Clanricarde estates. Mr. Michael Davitt summarizes the number of families that have been evicted, as follows:—"From 1846 to '48, (famine years) 240,000 families; from '48 to '80, 350,000 families; from '80 down to the present year, (1889) 10,000 families."

When we consider that the people have no resort to manufactures or public works, but must depend entirely on the produce of the land for subsistence, it is impossible to imagine the horrors those evictions must have entailed. "Around the poorest cabin," eloquently writes Mr. Davitt, "cling and cluster the tenderest feelings of the human heart;* within their rugged walls, the best and holiest of our affections have been exercised; memory holds fast to these abodes of the poor, and gives them a sanctity that ought, in a christian county, to be their shield and protection."

Lord Hartington, in his address to the people of Accrington, said "There was nothing in Ireland for the past two or three years but lawless agitation, caused by the confiscation of the tenants' improvements;" whilst J. A. Froude wrote, "Landlords in Ireland, for the most part, were aliens in blood and in religion; they represented conquest and confiscation, with an indifference to the welfare of the people, which would not have been tolerated in England or Scotland."

* "Ad ogni uccello, suo nido e bello."
  "To every bird its own nest is charming."

NOTE. A majority of rack-rented farms in Ireland are owned by absentee English landlords or London Corporations, such as "The Fishmongers, the Skinners, Ironmongers, Mercers, Salters, the Drapers;" the latter company own 27,025 acres whose valuation is £14,859.

CHAPTER VIII.

NOT only have Irish Catholics been unjustly deprived of their lands, or *rack-rented* when they were allowed to retain them, but they have been debarred from every lucrative office that was a gift of the government. In 1833, Mr. Lecky, writing of his time, declared "There was not in Ireland a single Catholic Judge, or stipendiary Magistrate; all the High Sheriffs, with one exception, and an overwhelming majority of the unpaid magistrates and of the Grand Jury; the five Inspectors General, and the thirty-two Sub-Inspectors of police were Protestants. The chief towns were, for the most part, in the hands of narrow-minded, corrupt and intensely bigoted corporations. Even in the Whig government, not a single Irishman had a seat in the Cabinet; the Irish Secretary's imperious manner and unbridled temper made him intensely hated. For many years promotion was withheld from those who advocated Catholic Emancipation, and the majority of the people found their bitterest enemies in the foremost places. Sir Gavan Duffy, in his "History of the Union" wrote: "In Ulster, there were 1100 magistrates; of these, scarcely a dozen were Catholics; very often the entire bench and its servants were members of an Orange Lodge."

The condition of the judiciary and government offices

is not much better at present. Mr. J. Balfour, and his uncle Lord Salisbury, Prime Minister of England, are notorious opponents of every scheme that has been devised to ameliorate the condition of Ireland. They invited Tory influence to reject Gladstone's Land Bill, and Mr. Parnell's Amendments, insisting on fixity of tenure, and the erasure of arrears. They introduced the Coercion Act, of 1886, which placed Ireland under a state of siege. No Coercion Act heretofore devised by the British Government involved such tyrannical and oppressive provisions. Besides embracing the quintessence of all previous repressive acts, it dispensed with trial by jury. While other penal acts were of a temporary durance, this statute was framed to continue in force until abrogated by positive legislation. Superior officers of the constablery, entirely ignorant of the principles of jurisprudence, and many of doubtful repute, were constituted *"removables,"* with power to decide all cases of alleged conspiracies, boycottings and agrarian outrages. These were authorized to transfer the venue from one district to another, even from Ireland to England, if they considered the case of the Crown prejudiced. The act created new crimes. At present, it is not a mere infraction of law, but a crime, a *criminal conspiracy*, for a man to attend a Land-League meeting in a proclaimed district. In the lord-lieutenant was vested the authority to proclaim a district or county, in fact he could proclaim the whole island if he pleased. Frequently meetings have been proclaimed but twenty-four hours antecedent to the time specified for their assemblage, thus furnishing a menacing incentive to the people to resist. In all the parish churches in proclaimed districts throughout Ireland, policemen are deputed to watch the congregation after Mass, lest they should engage in league meetings. Priests have been frequently arrested at their church doors and followed for miles, while discharging their missionary duties. Father McFadden of Gweedore was arrested just as he had retired from the altar where he had officiated. Although he could be seen a hundred times a day on other occasions, yet the most offensive and inopportune moment when he and his flock were leaving the church, was that selected for his arrest. Although Father McFadden* did his utmost to appease the fury of the populace, enraged at his arrest, he was, nevertheless, indicted by the government for complicity in the murder of Inspector Martin (Feb., 1889). As numerous other instances of Priest-hunting have occurred since the passage of the Coercion Act of '86, our brief narrative will only permit the insertion of a few of the most remarkable and ludicrous.

During the past year a popular young Priest was tracked by a policeman the entire way from his church to a lady's private residence some three miles distant. He forced his way through the hall, and thence to the drawing room where he met the Priest and the astonished landlady who asked him the meaning of his visit. He nonchalantly replied that he presumed a Land-League meeting was to be held there. A military captain in Birr, King's Co., commanded his regiment to leave the church while Father P. Brennan was preaching to his congregation. Rev. R. Little, a respectable

* The people of Memphis, Tenn., will be pleased to learn that this noble clergyman is a brother of the late Chief McFadden, one of the yellow fever martyr heroes of 1878. See Heroes and Heroines of Memphis, page 60.

Clare parish Priest, avers that whenever he attends sick calls, two constables follow him and await his return to the parsonage. As this Priest has frequently outwitted the constablery, holding meetings almost within the shadow of their helmets, a mounted policeman, for whose support the barony is taxed, is especially deputed to watch his nocturnal movements. In almost every parish police note takers report all words spoken that are supposed to have a political bias in favor of the National League. Very Rev. Canon Keller and Rev. M. Ryan were sentenced to hard labor imprisonment for refusing to reveal in court monetary and other political secrets confided to them by their respective flocks. Rev. Father Kennedy, of Meelin, Co. Cork, a very enlightened clergyman who spent the greater portion of his priestly career in England, was incarcerated three times. On the occasion of his last arrest, the police, without any previous warning whatever, broke into his residence at night and took him to jail, paying no attention to the condition of his health, enfeebled since his last imprisonment. This good clergyman avers that the only Crown pretext for his two first terms of imprisonment was an advice to his flock to use every lawful means to defend their homes during the process of eviction. It would be amusing, if it were not so painful, to listen to Father Kennedy glory in his victory over the prison officials who required him to exercise with thieves, pick-pockets and murderers; as also relate his ruse obtaining boiled eggs in a coffee kettle. Besides the afore mentioned, the following Priests have been imprisoned for terms ranging from two to eight months: Very Rev. Canons, Doyle and Brosnan, Revs. Stephens, Clarke, Maher, McCarthy, Sheehy, Marnan, Farrelly, O'Dwyer, (the latter was sentenced for eight months).

The ignominy of sentencing respectable clergymen to imprisonment for technical offenses was aggravated by their after treatment within the prison walls. Although the inhuman treatment of political prisoners had been denounced (in the pages of the Dublin Freeman of 1889) by many of the leading statesmen of Europe, America, and other civilized nations, still the Tory government obstinately refused to mitigate prison rigor in favor of political prisoners, or segregate them from exercising with the worst grades of criminals. Indeed, it savors political cowardice, if not petty savagery, that a great government, such as that of England, should connive at its minions stripping and almost strangling such dauntless patriots as William O'Brien, John Mandeville and Larkin in their efforts to substitute prison garb. To regulate prison discipline so as to sap the life and vigor of manhood, and render the victim fit only for the grave, comprises the guilt and malice of insidious manslaughter. Several political prisoners besides the stouthearted John Mandeville, died almost immediately after their liberation from prison. Many others would have undoubtedly shared the same fate, had not public opinion revolted against such barbarity. It is almost incredible that the alleged crimes for which these men were incarcerated and lost their lives (their advocacy of Nationalism) before the ratification of the Coercion Act of '86, were not considered crimes at all. Ever since the passage of this Coercion Bill, Nationalism is proscribed, so that to advocate or sympathize with Home Rule tactics incriminates a man and disqualifies him for every office that is the gift of the government. No Nationalists, now-a-days, need apply for positions in Customs, Excise, Coast or Navy Service, Bank of Ireland or Post Office. Even the rural post offices in the wildest districts are invariably bestowed on Protestants and anti-Nationalists.* In the village of Tulla, Co. Clare, consisting of some six thousand inhabitants, and not more than twenty-five Protestants, the post office is in the hands of an uncompromising Tory bigot. In the little hamlet of Lisdoonvarna, (west Clare), where there are not five Protestants against a thousand Catholics, a young Miss of fifteen (a Protestant) has charge of the post office and telegraph station. Last summer ('89) a young man had to be sent from Dublin to initiate her in the manipulation of telegraphy, the position being withdrawn from an experienced gentleman, but a reputed Nationalist. Although this young lady mislaid many of my letters during her postal novitiate, it is due to her to say that her manners and features are very agreeable, and now that she is duly installed, we would be sorry to hear of her dismissal.

Few Irishmen, in these days, are entitled to add J. P. (Justice of Peace) to their names. The majority have to be content with T. C. (Town Council), M. B. C. (Member of Bicycle Club), or P. L. G. (Poor Law Guardian), which has been ludicrously rendered Poor Lame Gander.

* In Cootehill (Cavan), out of the eleven paid officials of the workhouse, there is but one Catholic, although three-fourths of the rate payers are Catholics. Last October, 1889, when a nurse was required, an inexperienced Protestant girl was installed, although 95 per cent. of the sick poor are Catholics.

CHAPTER IX.

POLICE UBIQUITY AND ESPIONAGE.

A STRANGER visiting Ireland at present, would imagine the country to be in an actual state of warfare. There is a constabulary mansion erected within an average radius of every three miles throughout the length and breadth of the populated portion of the whole island. These buildings which are decidedly the neatest and most costly in their vicinity, contain from ten to twenty-five men each. Besides these, there are countless police huts improvised for the accommodation and protection of land-gentry and their agents who have made themselves obnoxious in the eyes of the tenantry. Members of the constablery are also drafted to replace families who have been evicted from their homesteads. Every district is taxed *pro rata* for the maintenance of emergency men and extra police, in such a manner that the landlords are exempt, while the tenant farmers are held responsible.

Mr. John Ellis, M. P., declared before the House of Commons (Dec., '88), "That if the government ruled Ireland with a respectable regard for the wishes of the people, it would save £1,000,000 ($5,000,000) it was then expending on the constablery."* In 1871, the expenses of the force were 3s. 4d. per head; in '76, 3s. 11d.; in '81, 4s. 7d., and in 1888, 6s. per head. These

---

* "The Government," says John Dillon, M. P., "expends £1,500,000 a year for police, and but £800,000 for education."

figures only refer to country districts. To estimate the amount of municipal police tax, one instance will suffice.

In the city of Limerick there are seven constabularies and five military barracks, the latter being the *rendezvous* for more than a thousand soldiers. The almost interminable lines of infantry and cavalry that may be seen each morning marching or drilling in glittering uniform warrant the assumption of rebellion or hostile invasion. We venture to assert that Limerick, with 38,000 inhabitants, scarcely sufficient to require municipal franchise, has within its precincts more constablery and military than Chicago with its million inhabitants.

Policeman are so engrossed with castle espionage that they frequently fail to arrest disorderly or drunken men in the public streets. Although to a stranger it is inexplicable, yet it is a notorious fact that in those localities where the League of the Cross has been established, policemen chiefly abound. If by such policy, the Chief Secretary aims at political capital, he might outrival the Prince of Darkness. In every civilized country, policemen are, *ex-officio*, friendly towards the populace; in Ireland, they are the avowed enemies of the people, and in numerous instances, paid spies of the British government.* Their promotion entirely depends on the cubic measure of their anti-Nationalist prejudice.

* Although apparently preposterous, it has been frequently observed that even domestic animals seem to hold the Irish police in disdain; while little and large dogs incessantly snarl or bark as they approach and pass, the Irish gander seldom fails to make an impression on the nether extremities of some constable in Her Majesty's service. This notorious aversion to the constabulary probably afforded a theme for the popular but proscribed ballad entitled "The Peeler and the Goat."

Who has not heard of the famous, or rather infamous Judge William Keough? This apostate patriot with John Sadlier (a London merchant) actually concocted the most dangerous secret society ever known in Ireland, the "Finian Brotherhood." This society was subsequently organized (in 1858) by John Mitchell, James Stephens and O'Meagher. From the position of constable, Keough, after his apostasy, was raised to the Judge's bench; before whom, in 1865, some of the first Finian organizers, Messrs. Luby, O'Leary and O'Donovan Rossa were *tried* and condemned to life-long penal servitude. The wily Peter O'Brien, designated by the ignoble sobriquet of "Peter the Packer," was promoted Judge, from being an insignificant barrister, and recently "Lord Chief Justice," for his jury-packing proclivities. Avowed hostility to the national cause is the only ostensible qualification for the preferment of Judges Litton, Webb and Kisley. Judge Waters who has recently reversed some *"removable"* sentences, has hereby debarred himself from any position in the privy council or lord-lieutenant's household. Cols. Foster, Clifford-Lloyd, (Cecil-Roche), Turner and a thousand other political mushrooms have been selected by the government for their antiseptic abhorrence of Home Rule.

At every railway station in Ireland, two or more policemen are deputed to watch all in-coming and outgoing trains. Unlike the English, and indeed all well regulated constablery, they bear no numbers, so that their identity, in case of their conduct being questioned, cannot be established. Many police officers receive extravagant pay in lieu of a bribe, to induce them to perform deeds hostile to their countrymen. Hence, on frequent occasions, they have wantonly insulted and truncheoned harmless citizens, intruded themselves into private dwellings, and disturbed Catholic worship. Were it not for the interference of the Priests and the tolerant attitude recommended by Mr. Parnell and his colleagues, the people would have long since resisted. And in case they should resist, the police were empowered, (as they have frequently done) to fire and kill indiscriminately. Baron Dowse himself (a bitter opponent of Home Rule) protested against the unnecessary violence and ridiculous espionage of the Irish constablery. In Nov., '88, an Irish constable (Sullivan) had the hardihood to serve a writ of summons on the honorable David Sheehy, M. P., within the precincts of the House of Commons. At Fermoy, Miltown-Malbay and other places, it was attested in court that the police were endeavoring to purchase goods for the purpose of forcing the shop keepers to violate the law by their refusal. The infamous informer Cullinan is still in the police force. Mr. Ellis, M. P., proved to the House of Commons that the Irish tax payers were paying £400 ($2,000) a week for the extraordinary service of the constablery at evictions. The expenses of extra police in Lord Clanricarde's estate amount to £1,700 a year; the county Clare alone was mulcted £6,000. A compensative tax has been levied for the widows of Inspector Martin and Constable Whelehan who organized the Sexton outrage. The extra police tax for the year 1886, amounted to £53,493. In December, '88, during the Parnell Commission, an Irishman named Pat Molloy was summoned before the commissary judges. It transpired during the cross-examination, that the government officials believed that this Molloy was the same individual of the name who was implicated in the

Phoenix Park assassination. An agent of the London *Times* was sent to him for the purpose of extorting a confession. Molloy, dissimulating his identity, insinuated that he could reveal astounding secrets, inculpating Parnell, Davitt, and prominent Leaguers. He refused to accompany the *Times'* agent to London until he had secured eleven pounds which he said he owed, and must pay before leaving Ireland. Having received the money, he immediately sent five pounds of it to the Parnell Fund. When reproached by Attorney General Webster for having thus deceived the agent, he laconically retorted: "He tried to entrap me, I succeeded in trapping him."

NOTE. For this offence, Molloy was sentenced to six months' imprisonment.

CHAPTER X.

THE LAND OR NATIONAL LEAGUE, BOYCOTTING, Etc.

THE Irish people, seeing that the government failed to sympathize with their national aspirations, and having learned from experience, that Gladstone's Land Bill and Compensation Act did not retrieve their past, or allay their present grievances, were naturally disposed to lend themselves to any movement which purported to insure the maintenance and ratification of their rights.

Being, however, descended from ancestors who had submitted to untold cruelties in opposing every measure that conflicted with their national faith, they were consequently averse to associations disapproved or condemned by Catholic authority. Hence, only apostate or luke warm Catholics cared to enroll themselves members of secret or oath-bound confraternities, such as *Finianism, Ribbonism, Whiteboyism*, and later on *Clan-na-Gaels*. These physical Force Associations never found favor with a majority of the Irish people.

It was otherwise with organizations that had the approval of the Catholic church and clerical coöperation. The Land or National League was such an institution. In 1879, there existed in Dublin a Tenants' Defence Association, who inscribed on their programme the three famous F's: free sale, fair rent, and fixity of tenure. This association was first established at Ballinasloe, Co. Galway, by Mr. Mathew Harris. It must be remembered that Gladstone's Land Bill did not include fixity of tenure; it also failed to notice the condition of arrears. Hence, landlords taking advantage of these covert, or rather *overt* omissions, have evicted by thousands, insolvent tenants, as also tenants who had been in arrears. The first germ of the Land League might be said to have sprung from the Dublin branch. The Land League proper, or the League systematically organized was first established at Irishtown, Co. Galway, by Mr. Michael Davitt, aided by Mr. Brennan, October 22d, 1879. Mr. Davitt, universally acknowledged the "Father" of the Land League, an ex-convicted Finian, was the son of a poor farmer who was dispossessed from his homestead while he was yet a child. Although not nominally implicated in the allegations of "Parnellism and Crime," nevertheless, he defended his own case before the Commission, concluding with an oration whose depth and eloquence elicted the approbation of the Commissary Judges.

Mr. Charles Stewart Parnell,[*] the acknowledged head of the Home Rule party, impersonating the ardor of the Celt and sagacity of the Saxon, has been a staunch advocate and promoter of the National League. A native of Ireland (Avondale, Co. Wicklow) of Anglo-Saxon descent, and a Protestant, he is justly regarded

---

[*] Mr. C. S. Parnell is a descendant of the English poet Parnell, and of John and Henry Parnell who stoutly supported Grattan in his struggles against the Union. He is the recognized head of the Home Rule party. He was elected a member of the House of Commons in 1875.

one of the first statesmen of the British empire. Besides his obstructive policy in the House of Commons, his shrewd avoidance of political traps set to ensnare him, would lead one to believe that the *Stars* as well as the *Graces* connived at his diplomacy. At the first Land League meeting he attended (1879) at Westport, he openly advised the tenants to let the landlords see they intended to keep a *"firm grip of the land."* These words, though of monosyllabic simplicity, were subsequently inscribed in the banner of the League, and were destined to be the death-knell of landlordism.

In a very short time, branches of the League were established in every parish and district throughout Ireland. The land movement became amazingly popular with peasant and citizen, rich and poor.* In furtherance of the movement, Mr. Parnell, accompanied by Mr. John Dillon, M. P., decided to go to America. Their reception in the States was a series of enthusiastic ovations. At Washington, the House of Representatives, by a derogation of rule heretofore without precedent, authorized the Irish Delegates to address the House. Financially, their tour was even more successful. Three hundred and sixty thousand dollars were subscribed, and entrusted to Mr. Parnell. This amount was mostly expended on those who had suffered from the famine which prevailed at the time.

Lest the reader should confuse the Land League, the National League and Home Rule associations, it is pertinent to premise they are synonymical terms. When the Land League was proscribed by the government, by

---

* Branches of the Land League were established in every important city of England, Scotland, America and Australia.

way of subterfuge, it assumed the name of "National League;" whilst the first articles in the constitution of both Leagues advocated national autonomy or Home Rule for Ireland. It was this latter phase of the League's character that rendered it so detestable in the estimation of the Tories. The popularity of the Land League and Home Rule movement was not confined to Ireland. Some of the greatest statesmen of England and Scotland ranked themselves with the Parnellites. The ex-prime Minister of England, W. E. Gladstone, the ex-Viceroy of Ireland, Earl Spencer, the orator and distinguished historian, John Morley, M. P., the Journalist Labouchére, M. P., and a galaxy of other great English diplomats, espoused the cause of self government for Ireland.

In mentioning the chief promoters of the League in Ireland it would be unjust to omit the names of Archbishops Walsh of Dublin, Croke of Cashel, Loague of Armagh and MacEvelly of Tuam. Indeed, the efficiency of the Episcopate and Priesthood should never be forgotten in the annals of Irish patriotism. Their influence contributed much towards keeping the fire of patriotism burning in the heart of the nation. While we thus give superior credit to the Irish clerisy, it would be unjust to conceal or ignore the supreme merits of the secular patriots, amongst whom we shall especially mention, besides the aforementioned leaders, Parnell, Davitt, Dillon, Brennan and Harris, Mr. Redmond, Mr. Joseph Biggar (a Belfast merchant), Messrs. Harrington, Sexton, a native of Waterford, and ex-Mayor of Dublin, Mr. Wm. O'Brien and Hon. T. D. Sullivan, whose songs "God save Ireland," "Murty Hines," and "A Toast to Old Ireland," are incorporated amongst the nation's souvenirs.

After the insertion of Home Rule, the minor articles of the Land League constitution inculcated Mr. Parnell's caution "To *keep a firm grip of the land;*" to exercise every lawful resistance in defence of homestead, and under no circumstances to lease or occupy land from which a tenant was unjustly evicted. Land-grabbing was to be regarded as the foulest stain that could tarnish the national escutcheon. An intruder, occupying a tenant's house or farm, was to be socially ostracised or *Boycotted*, a word borrowed from the name of the first victim who was excommunicated by the League.

It was against the spirit of the League to buy from, sell to, or associate with, a boycotted person, except where his life was jeopardized. Each member of the League was required to contribute a monthly, or bi-monthly instalment; besides, he was frequently taxed to contribute other dues, when extraordinary occasions demanded them. This money was deposited in a central fund, located in Dublin (Mr. T. Harrington was treasurer in '89), and was chiefly used for the support of evicted tenants, the building of improvised huts for their shelter, &c. In Land-League meetings crime of every nature and grade was severely denounced. Parnellites regarded the commission of social and agragrian crimes the severest attacks on their policy.* That nothing criminal or immoral should be tolerated by the League is evident from the fact that most of its branches were directed by Priests of acknowledged prudence and probity. In rural districts few of the peasantry were capable

---

* Mr. Parnell, when first apprized of the Phoenix Park assassination, was so horrified that he contemplated resigning the leadership of the Home Rule party.

of presiding over such assemblies; men who spent their lives in the field or farm could not be expected to be expert in parliamentary rules and by-laws. Hence, when and wherever available, Priests were elected to the chair, being more eligible by reason of their education, as also their influence in suppressing petty quarrels and jealousies that frequently occurred in and out of such meetings. Indeed, many of the League branches would have disbanded, or segregated into various political cliques, if it were not for the efficient coöperation of the Priesthood.

N. B. The central branch of the League was empowered tô decide the questions of all agrarian difficulties, and when advisable, to suspend or rescind any recalcitrant branch.

Chapter XI.

THE PLAN OF CAMPAIGN AND PAPAL RESCRIPT.

THE numerous cruel evictions that took place in recent years for the non-payment of arrears and impossible rents induced several Irish tenant-farmers to adopt defensive, if not retaliative measures against their oppressors. Under such auspices, Mr. John Dillon, M. P., invented the famous Plan of Campaign in the autumn of 1886. Descended from chivalrous and high born ancestry, this impassioned orator almost outrivalled Mr. Parnell in the hearts of the Irish people. Seeing the apathy and inability of the land-court to grapple with agrarian grievances, he advised the tenants to combine for a reduction of rent, and the reinstatement of evicted tenants. The Plan struck the key-note of Irish enthusiasm, and soon became the offensive and defensive watch-word of the peasantry in every barony of the nation. Its efficiency surprised both victors and victims. However, when its primitive weapons are carefully examined, it appears that the Plan differs from old Land-League combinations, merely in detail, but not in principle.

The tenants who join the Plan deposit their rents in what is technically called the *"War Chest"*--they hand over their rents to some trust worthy neighbor—frequently, to the Priest of the parish who retains the funds thus confided to him, until the difficulty between landlord and tenant is adjusted. Those who prove false to the "Plan" forfeit the moneys they deposited. The Plan is called into action where one or more tenants have been unjustly evicted, or when a reasonable reduction of rent demanded, is refused by the landlord. In such, and similar cases, the tenants pay no rent until their demands or deserts are complied with. Father Mathew Ryan and Mr. Thomas Moroney of Herbertstown, Co. Limerick, were the first persons committed to prison for court contempt (the latter was kept in jail twenty-four months) for refusing to divulge the location of the "War Chest."

It is scarcely a metaphor to say that, for a time, the Plan set the Irish heart on fire, and that Mr. William O'Brien was its most formidable firebrand. We have too much respect, however, for this eloquent, and we might say martyr-patriot, to insinuate that he exercised his influence without reason or cause, for he had both; although his frail body is little better than a human shell, yet the ardor of his eloquence prevailed and was justly applauded by sympathizers, not only at home, but throughout England, Scotland, Australia and Canada.

As the moral features of the Plan of Campaign and Boycotting have been questioned by the highest authority in the Catholic church, it will be interesting to know why both, at present, are tolerated by the clergy and maintained by the Irish people, who have never swerved from their adhesion to Catholic doctrine. At first sight it would appear that the Plan directly militates against that freedom necessary to constitute a lawful contract, whilst Boycotting seems to infringe on the exercise of human liberty.

Since this is a very delicate question, few critics being capable of advancing a reliable decision, we doubt if our solution will prove satisfactory, especially when it is understood that some of the leading theologians in Ireland and elsewhere entertain conflicting, if not opposite opinions on this subject. It has been maintained that the Plan of Campaign in no wise differs from the "*Trades Unions*" of England and America. But let us discuss the question by first examining an actual, rather than a hypothetical case, viz: Mr. Ponsonby, or Lord Clanricarde owns an estate consisting of several thousand acres which are sub-let to a certain number of tenant-farmers who pay a certain rent. That the owner should have a right to demand rent, or sell his lands to whom he please, is the dictate of common justice.

This mooted land question must be divided into *legal* and *moral* ownership; the landlords have unquestionably a legal title; the tenants claim a moral title which they consider unlawful to ignore or confiscate.

We admit, there is little or no hesitation about evicting an insolvent tenant in England or America. The sheriff immediately dispossesses him. It is different in Ireland, for the reason there is a *dual* ownership in the land. Tenants who improve land worth only five shillings an acre (when first occupied) to a condition which rendered it worth twenty-five shillings an acre, consider they have a right to the fruit of their industry. Land improvement may occur in various ways, viz: by draining, fencing, fertilizing, building upon, etc. Irish families regard it unwarranted confiscation to sell their property or evict them from farms which they, and possibly three generations of their ancestors, drained, fenced, fertilized and built upon. In numerous cases,

Irish farmers have large families; they seldom work outside their own holdings; they justly believe the landlord should appreciate, and remunerate them for their united toil. Instead of rewarding however, landlords in the past have invariably advanced their rentals commensurate with the tenants' improvements, thus obliging them to purchase their own industry. Eviction stared them unless they complied, at least in part, leaving impossible ARREARS in the land agent's books, a legacy that forced thousands, yea, hundreds of thousands to emigrate to Australia and America.

We allow, the newly constituted Land Courts have made considerable reductions in rent, but it was not native benevolence that induced them, but the Plan of Campaign that *forced* them to these desperate concessions. Recently, when the price of stock advanced in Ireland, the land commissioners refused to lower the rents; an event which induced the Irish Bishops, Doctor McCarthy, the veteran Bishop of Cloyne, and Dr. Fitzgerald, to write to Mr. Lane, M. P., (Jan. 28, '89) complaining of the judgment of the land commissioners. Mr. John Dillon, M. P., in a recent speech said "That as soon as the Tory government came into power, they authorized Lord Londonderry to appoint land commissioners." Although ostensibly indifferent, this is really a vituperative sarcasm; for Lord Londonderry* is an unsavory landlord himself, having had much difficulties with his tenantry. Considering these adjuncts, it is too much to expect of human nature, that this peer should be an impartial umpire in the appointment of trustworthy commissioners. Under such circumstances, the

---

* This peer owns 30,000 acres in Ireland.

tenant-farmers, having no impartial tribunal to which they might appeal, felt they had only one resource left, self-defence in the Plan of Campaign. Rather than go to the poor house or emigrant ship, (the latter not always available) they felt that they were not sinning against divine or natural law in combining to resist those who threatened to rob them of their lands, their homes, and the fruit of their life long industry.

For similar reasons they exercised Boycotting against land grabbers or selfish cormorants who took evicted farms, since their action was the fellest stroke against their self-defensive attitude.

THE PAPAL RESCRIPT.

Owing to repeated complaints sent to Rome, many of which were under the tutelage of the Duke of Norfolk and Lord Errington, the present Pope Leo XIII sent over to Ireland a distinguished member of the papal household, Mons. Persico, to examine the difficulties that existed between the British government and the Land League. It has been stated, that being misled by castle influence, he reported adversely to the national cause. In either event, His Holiness issued a rescript, addressed to the Bishops of Ireland, condemning Boycotting and the Plan of Campaign. The Hierarchy and people of Ireland received it with all the deference due to a papal mandate, but contended that it was obtained by misrepresentation, and that in any event its damnatory clauses were conditional, and that the objectionable features reported did not exist in the Plan of Campaign or policy of the Irish leaders. Hence, the Irish Hierarchy, with the exception of Dr. O'Dwyer, Bishop of Limerick, were reticent in regard to the rescript.

M. De Pressensé, in his recent history, L' Irlande et l'Angletèrre, (page 552) repeats what O'Connell once ventured to assert, "That although the Irish people are willing to receive *religious*, they are not disposed to receive *political* instruction from Rome."

CHAPTER XII.

IRISH JURIES AND COURTS OF JUSTICE.

WHETHER there are impartial and justly constituted courts wherein the people can find redress, as the Papal Rescript insinuated, may be seen from a perusal of the following evidence. His Lordship, the Bishop of Raphoe, writing to Mr. Gray, Editor of the Dublin "Freeman," regarding the trial of Father McFadden, and others charged with the murder of Inspector Martin, made the following indictment:

LETTERKENNY, 28th October, 1889.

DEAR MR. GRAY:—What you state of the conduct of the prosecution at Maryborough is, I regret to say, only too true. The worst anticipations of the Archbishops have come to pass. Their just protests, in the interests of a fair trial, against straining the forms of law to secure a conviction at any cost, have been treated with silent contempt at every stage; for the principles these protests embody have been steadily ignored. The prisoners are taken to a far distance from their homes for trial among utter strangers; they are not being tried by a jury of their peers, but by a special jury of the Queen's County; and on the special jury their religion is practically banned. With panels of convenient length to draw upon, the Crown can select a jury to its own liking, and Catholics obviously are not up to the taste of those who at present represent the Crown.

✠ PATRICK O'DONNELL.

Regarding the tampering of juries, a Mr. Smellie, an Englishman and a Protestant, inserted the following complaint in last year's "Dublin Freeman" (1889):

"In the question which Mr. MacDonald put to the Chief Secretary last Thursday, he mentioned my name as the special juror at Maryborough Assizes who, after he had been sworn to try the Kerry murder case, said in open court, "I object to try a man for his life on a packed jury;" and Mr. Balfour said in his reply that as I had found a verdict against Hickey I appeared to have changed my mind. I beg to contradict this. My mind is still the same as when I made my protest to the judge. I object to try a man for his life on a packed jury. I maintain that the jury was packed. It consisted of eleven Protestants and only one Catholic. It is true we found a verdict against Hickey in accordance with the evidence, but this does not prove that the jury was not packed. I consider it a gross insult that every second man on the special jury panel should be ordered to "stand aside," and I say it is not only insulting to the special jurors but it is an outrage on the British constitution of which the jury system is a gem. I am an Englishman and a Protestant, of over thirty-seven years residence in Ireland, and I have observed since the last Coercion Act was passed that jury-packing has been systematically carried out in Maryborough, particularly in those cases where the venue has been changed. Those who uphold this system seem entirely to forget that in order to govern wisely we must above all things govern justly. How can we expect loyalty from an Irishman treated in this way when narrow-minded officials have power to strain and pervert them."

When the Attorney-General, Sir Richard Webster, asked Mr. Wm. O'Brien, M. P., why he did not denounce crime in Ireland, the latter replied before the Parnell Commissioners "That it was impossible to determine what was, and what was not crime in Ireland, since the whole administration was in the hands of two infamous men; one, the chief director of the detective department, was sentenced for a variety of crimes; the other was fined $40,000 for cruelty and injustice to his wife."

Hon. Thomas Sexton, M. P., in his exposure of the nefarious methods used in the oppression of the Irish race, says of the Irish National League: "A cause with such a record cannot fail; the best faculties of our own race have been expended in its service, the best blood of our people has been shed in its behalf, men have served the cause who have made the prison cell a shrine of fame and the scaffold a place of honor."

We will enumerate a few further examples of alleged "Law and Order" in Ireland:

1. The following evidence of jury-packing was submitted by Mr. T. M. Healy, M. P., and appeared in the Dublin "Freeman" of '89:

"In the case of a Thomas Higgins, fifty-four Catholic jurors were rejected, and the prisoner declared 'guilty;' in the case of Pat Higgins, also found 'guilty,' forty were rejected; in the case of Pat Joyce (hanged) thirty-nine; in the case of Joe Poole (hanged) forty-seven; in the case of Francis Hines (hanged) twenty-six; in the case of Miles Joyce (hanged) twenty-eight jurors were ordered to stand aside, almost all being rejected on account of their Catholicity."

2. During the Lough Mask trial, when the jury found

a verdict of "guilty" against Mr. Pat Higgins, one of three indicted for murder, Judge O'Brien (now Chief Justice O'Brien) prejudiced the case of the two remaining prisoners by announcing before the jury " I consider it my duty that I believe the convicted prisoner to be the least culpable of those indicted for this murder."

3. In Pressensé's l'Irlande et l'Angletèrre, (page 441), we read: "Two hundred men were sworn in to decide a certain case under the Crimes Act. The list presented nine Catholics to one Protestant; the Crown solicitor succeeded in rejecting the Catholics, substituting a jury consisting of eleven Protestants and one Catholic."

4. The same author states (page 412) that, in numerous cases, prisoners accused of capital crimes, were brought before tribunals and condemned, whilst as far as they were cognizant, their trial and accusation might have been conducted in Hebrew, since they only spoke the Celtic tongue, and had no interpreter. One of the prisoners being informed in court of his conviction, exclaimed, "It is a slaughter house."

The Pall-Mall Gazette, commenting on this conviction, stated: "No impartial person can deny that, in this case, there has been jury-packing and oppression which would not be tolerated in England."

And, here we would observe that, if an article such as the above, appeared in an Irish newspaper, the editor would be prosecuted for libel.

5. The late Mr. Ed. Dwyer Gray, editor of the Dublin "Freeman" having made some comments on the exclusion of Catholics from juries, and referring to certain members of a jury who were drunk the night before they found a verdict of "guilty" against the accused,

was mulcted by Judge Lawson the sum of £500 ($2,500).

6. Mr. William O'Brien, M. P., editor of "United Ireland," was sued for seditious libel under the provisions of an obsolete code of Edward III; whilst a Mr. Denis McNamara, a respectable shopkeeper of Ennis, Co. Clare, was imprisoned for advertising on his shop window, the sale of "United Ireland."

7. Mr. Foster, when Chief Secretary of Ireland, endeavored to convict the leaders of the ladies' Land League under another obsolete statute of Edward III, enacted chiefly against prostitutes and vagabonds. Having failed in this attempt, Mr. Clifford Lloyd succeeded in convicting Miss Kirk to three months imprisonment, and the Misses McCormack, Reynold, Moore and Mary O'Connor to six months each. Since they could not in common decency, be charged under the statute of Edward III, they were condemned for intimidation. Their intimidation consisted in their devoting a portion of their League funds towards the erection of huts for evicted tenants. While in prison, these respectable ladies were closeted in their cells during twenty-two hours of each day, being allowed only two hours' fresh air and exercise. (Pressensé).

8. During the process of an eviction on the land of a Mr. Blake, a young girl, named Ellen McDonough, and an old woman of sixty-five, a Mrs. Deare, were mortally wounded by the police. The jury returned a verdict of wilful murder against certain constables, yet no punishment followed.

9. Oct. 5, 1889. A Tipperary district Inspector, surrounded by some twenty policemen, ordered a certain constable to fire on a crowd of unarmed boys who were

amusing themselves on the street. One of the number, was instantly killed. The coroner's jury returned the following verdict: "That the said Stephen Heffernan met his death by a wound inflicted by constable Tuohey, of the R. I. C.; and we find that John Colles Carter, district Inspector, did aid, counsel, and direct said John Tuohey to commit wilful, felonious and malicious killing." As might be expected, no conviction or punishment followed.

10. Sergeant Jas. Beyers, R. I. C., fired at a fishing boat which was sailing on the river Bann. The owner of the boat, Jas. Robinson, his son and a Mr. Campbell (Nationalists) accompanied by the parish Priest deliberately swore that they saw the sergeant fire three shots at the boat. The sergeant alone, testified that the whole charge was a fabrication. The jury, after some deliberation, dismissed the case. But this is not the end. The Crown has commenced proceedings against these three men for perjury, and will undoubtedly convict them before an Armagh jury. (Dublin Freeman, Oct., '89).

11. "Dublin Freeman," Nov. 10, '89. Ladies summoned for laughing. A Tipperary correspondent says that on Tuesday, the police there were busily engaged serving summonses on a number of most respectable young ladies, commanding them to answer a charge of riotous behavior which, it is alleged, consisted of a laugh given at the police who were in the rear of a procession.*

---

* Last December, '89, a ballad singer and his wife were sentenced to three months' imprisonment for singing a ballad, entitled "We'll all go to Ireland when the landlords go."

12. Three English M. Ps., Messrs. Blunt, Harrison and Conybeare, were imprisoned, the former for publicly advocating the Plan of Campaign; the two latter for supplying food to a family who had re-entered their home from which they had been evicted.

We will waive further reference to these deplorable specimens of "Law and Order," by a resumé of the Parnell Judicial Commission.

13. THE PARNELL COMMISSION, (continued during 128 sessions, and ending November 22d, 1889).

A careful reader of the reports of this long and wearisome investigation, cannot fail to regard it as a judicial farce, instituted for political purposes chiefly aiming to crush Parnellite influence and suppress Home Rule aspirations.

Before the Commissary Judges sat, Sir William Harcourt, then Secretary of State of the Interior, relying solely on informer Carey's evidence, did not hesitate to boast that "he would take the *starch* out of the boys," meaning Parnell and his colleagues. Mr. Foster expected to implicate Mr. Parnell as a moral accomplice in the Phoenix Park assassination (of Cavendish and Burke, May 6, '82). Hence, as early as the 6th of May, '83, he insinuated before the House of Commons, that Mr. Parnell was an accomplice. The London "Times," commenting on Mr. Foster's accusation, stated: "The severe accusation of Mr. Foster had fallen on Mr. Parnell like the blow of a whip on a man's face." The Irish Nation revolted against the charge, and in evidence of their resentment, prepared a testimonial headed by the patriotic Archbishop of Cashel, amounting to £40,000 ($200,000).

Direct as well as circumstantial evidence has shown

that Pigott, (the infamous forger) was not the only malicious abettor of "Parnellism and Crime."* It has been averred that he was but a tool employed to work out the destruction of the Irish party, and has been sarcastically insinuated that when he blew out his brains in Madrid, he revealed a more sensitive conscience than the "Times" who prosecuted without remorse or scruple. From cross-examination and other evidence, it has transpired that Mr. Houston, who purchased the Parnell-Egan letters for the "London Times," knew they were forgeries. The government appeared to be, and undoubtedly was, acting in collusion with the "Times" in the accusation of Mr. Parnell and his colleagues, by lending them their greatest barrister, Sir Richard Webster, the Attorney-General. His entire course of direct and cross-examination clearly evinced that he was not engaged to calmly investigate, but rather to rigorously *prosecute*. Accordingly, he prolonged his suit with all subtle tenacity and legal quibbling of a shrewd barrister and bigot. The evident bias of the President of the Commission, Sir James Hannan, and his associate Judges (Day and Smith) has been adversely commented upon by the Tory, as well as the liberal English press. They concurred with the advocates of the "Times," demanding a strict investigation of all Land League, Clan-na-Gael and I. R. B. associations, not only in Ireland, but in England, France and America. Agrarian crimes and outrages were unraveled as if the alleged perpetrators were on trial for their lives. Land League books, bank accounts and other

---

* Mr. Flanigan, son of Judge Flanigan, was the author of "Parnellism and Crime," first published in London Times, April 18, '87.

compromisory documents were exposed to the severest scrutiny. All this industry appeared to be devoted only to the Parnellite side of the question. When Sir Charles Russell (Parnell's eloquent advocate) demanded the inspection of the I. L. P. U. documents, they were withheld, by consent of the Judges. The government opened its prison doors and summoned some of the most notorious criminals, such as Delaney, and Farraher* to testify against Mr. Parnell and his associates. It is noteworthy that scarcely a respectable witness appeared in behalf of the "Times." Police constables of doubtful veracity, bailiffs, informers and spies of the Cary and Le Caron type were the chief witnesses subpœned by the "Times," and maintained in London for weeks and months at enormous expense. In the case of a Priest, (Rev. Peter Quinn, Tulla, Co. Clare) subpœned by the "Times," the Attorney-General failed to examine him, having learned that he intended to submit evidence hostile to the "Times." We have elsewhere noticed that a Mr. P. Molloy received eleven pounds for a vague promise of furnishing evidence calculated to sustain the case of "Parnellism and Crime;" whilst on the other hand, Mr. Ed. Harrington was severely mulcted for publishing in the "Kerry Sentinel" the recantation of the evidence of a "Times'" witness (O'Connor) who, in the presence of a Priest and Barrister, deposed on oath that he perjured himself in giving evidence before the Commission.

Pigott himself, while in Madrid, (under the assumed name of Ponsonby) sent a letter to London declaring

---

* Sentenced to penal servitude for life for complicity in the Phoenix Park assassination.

that his statements before the Commission were false, and that the letters purporting to be *fac similes* of Parnell's and Egan's handwriting were *forgeries* distorted from business letters of these gentlemen in his possession.* And, although Sir Charles Russell, (in his great six day speech) openly declared before the Commissary Judges that but for the *forged letters*, the libels of "Parnellism and Crime" would never have appeared, still the Commission continued to investigate, or rather prosecute, as antecedent and subsequent charges appeared to evince.

Several clerical dignitaries and ladies who appeared for Mr. Parnell, even Parnell himself, were, if not rudely, at least irrelevantly cross-examined.

The patent partiality of the Judges obliged Sir Charles Russell and Mr. Parnell to withdraw from the case. Although no verdict has yet been pronounced, yet the antecedent drift of judicial prejudice would lead us to expect a decision unfavorable to Mr. Parnell and the Irish cause. But the unbiased and intellectual world will decide in his favor; while those who have endeavored to crush his power and besmirch his name and the Nation's integrity, have politically and financially failed, Mr. Parnell and his colleagues have honorably succeeded.†

---

* These letters Pigott copied by tracing them over a window pane. The Parnell *fac similes*, (written nine years before) referred to the sale of Pigott's paper, "The Irishman."

† Whilst the manuscript of this little volume was in the hands of the printer, two very important events transpired.

1. The London "Times" (Feb. 3, '90) compromised with Mr. Parnell in his libel suit against the proprietors of that paper, allowing him damages amounting to £5,000 ($25,000), and £1,000 ($5,000) to

his Secretary, Mr. Henry Campbell; all expenses of the suit being paid by the "Times."

2. The Judges of the Parnell Commission (Feb. 13, '90) submitted to Parliament their final report. To the chagrin of the "Times" and Tories, they exonerated Mr. Parnell not only from complicity in the Phoenix Park assassination, (as implied in the forged letters of Pigott), but declared him innocent of the charges of direct or indirect incitement to crime and outrage. They likewise disproved the charges that while in Kilmainham prison Mr. Parnell knew that Sheridan and Boyton had been organizing outrage, and that he financially aided F. Byrne to escape to France. They, (the Judges) however, found Mr. Parnell, Mr. Davitt and some forty-four other Irish Representatives guilty of *criminal conspiracy* by their aiding and abetting boycotting, etc.

Here, we would respectfully request the reader to remember that acts heretofore reputed lawful, were declared criminal conspiracies by the Balfourian Coercion Act of '87. The Act, amongst other things, made it a criminal conspiracy for a farmer to attend a Land League meeting in a proclaimed district. Under a pretext as plausible, it might declare the act of kissing his wife, a *criminal conspiracy*.

CHAPTER XIII.

SYNOPSIS OF THE ALLEGED "UNION" BETWEEN GREAT BRITAIN AND IRELAND.

THE bribery and greed of English merchants and capitalists contributed to bring about what England was pleased to call the "Union," but what Ireland always justly regarded as a further disunion of popular sentiment and commercial interests. Sir Gavan Duffy, in his "History of the Union," and still more recently, the French historian, M. de Pressensé, have shown that the so-called "Union" of Great Britain and Ireland was an open fraud—a national farce—in which English gold and political intrigues played a winning part. Gladstone, in one of his great speeches advocating Irish autonomy, (1866) declared "There was no transaction in the history of nations more ignoble than the establishment of the 'Union' between Ireland and England." The historian Lecky ("Leaders of Public Life in Ireland," page 182) wrote of the "Union" that "There was nothing more dishonorable in English political history . . . the word honor appears to have no meaning in politics, if applied to Castlereagh or Pitt . . . the 'Union' as it was voted, was a crime of the deepest infamy, imposed on a people who, instead of demanding, openly protested against it, has vitiated public life in Ireland."

In 1800, O'Connell, addressing a meeting in Dublin, opposing the Act of "Union," said:—"Let every man who feels with me proclaim that if the alternative were offered to him of Union, or the re-enactment of the penal code, in all its pristine horrors, that he would prefer without hesitation the latter as the lesser and more sufferable evil; that he would rather confide in the justice of the Protestants, who have already liberated him, than lay his country at the feet of foreigners."

In 1844, before a jury entirely composed of Unionists, O'Connell declared without contradiction that £3,000,000 were expended to purchase the vote of the "Union." In the "Life of Grattan," by his son, this passage is found with reference to the means by which Lord Castlereagh destroyed the Irish Parliament—

"All that could be accomplished by gold or by iron, by bribes, or by threats, or by promises, was set in motion. Every effort was strained to bring round those who were disinclined, to seduce those who were hostile but necessitous, to terrify the timid and bear down the fearless, and those who had at heart the interest and independence of their country. The doors of the Treasury were opened, and a deluge of corruption covered the land. The Bench of Bishops, the Bench of Judges, the Bar, the Revenue, the army, the navy, civil offices, military and naval establishments, places, pensions, and titles were defiled and prostituted for the purpose of carrying the great Government object—this ill-omened Union."

When the "Union Act" was first proposed, a petition

bearing 707,000 names was forwarded to the House of Commons, whilst those who favored the "Union" could secure but 5,000 names. Lord Plunket, before he became Chancellor of Ireland, declared that if the "Union" were voted it would be *null* and *void*, and that no one would be bound to respect it. "I will," said he, "resist this measure to my last breath; and when my last hour approaches, I will lead my children, like Amilcar, before the Altar and make them vow eternal hostility to the destroyers of the liberty of their fatherland."

Sir George Ponsonby proposed this resolution before the House of Commons, in opposition to the "Union Act," "Resolved that the Irish Nation have a free and independent legislature, resident in the Kingdom, conformable to the definite arrangement of 1782." After a debate of 20 hours this motion was lost by a vote of only 106 against 105. Nine-tenths of the Irish people who lived before, and ever since the passage of the "Union Act" to the present day, have been opposed to such a constrained coalition.

The means employed to consummate the "Union" were of such a base and dubious character, that the son of the Duke of Portland burnt his father's papers relative to the period of his administration as Secretary of State. The Chancellor of Ireland, Lord Clare, Messrs. Wicham, King, Mardsden and the Knight of Kerry, who had been engaged promoting the "Union" also destroyed the State papers that referred to this event and epoch.

The Poynings Act* which required that every legislative act, voted by the Irish Parliament, should receive

---

* Passed at Drogheda, in 1494, under the auspices of Sir Ed. Poynings, Lord Deputy of Ireland.

the royal seal and be expedited in England, before the Viceroy could sanction it, had been the key-note of Irish legislature from the days of Henry VII. Although only one-seventh of the population were Protestant, still no Catholic had a seat in the House of Lords. Of 210 peers who possessed and exercised the voting franchise, 40 were English without a domicile in Ireland. In like manner, the House of Commons was exclusively recruited from Protestants. It is easy then to see from these antecedents how the rights and privileges of the Irish Nation were betrayed and bartered. The sentiments of an overwhelming majority of the inhabitants were ignored or disregarded. The same spirit still prevails. Except the Orange portion of the population, and a few isolated branches of the I. L. P. U., the entire population of the four provinces are opposed to the existent bastard "Union," on which the Imperial government never bestowed equal rights. But the clouds that lowered over the nation are gradually disappearing; whilst the rays of liberty's sunburst have already commenced to diffuse their effulgence over the North and South, the East and the West.

EFFECTS OF THE "UNION."

A vast plurality of the dying industries of Ireland began to decline from the passage and enforcement of this Act. The harbors of Cork and Galway, as also the fishing ports were neglected. Transatlantic shipping was completely monopolized by Liverpool, Bristol and Southampton. In 1727, an act prevailed in Ireland to encourage the use and manufacture of wool and linen. To encourage this industry the peasantry had the material of their under garments entirely composed of wool; they even clothed their dead in woolen raiment. They made similar efforts to promote the consumption of linen. At the funeral of Mr. Connolly, the Speaker of the Irish House of Commons, in 1729, the chief mourners appeared in linen scarves, a custom which is sacredly observed at funerals in Ireland to the present day. Soon after the Union, the manufacture of wool and flax was entirely abandoned throughout Ireland, except in Belfast, where the linen trade is still maintained.

In 1798, (immediately before the Union) Lord Clare wrote: "There is not a nation on the face of the habitable globe which has advanced in agriculture, manufacture and commerce, with the same rapidity, in the same period, as Ireland." In this same year, the Dublin bankers passed this resolution: "Resolved, that since the renunciation of the power of Great Britain in 1782, to legislate for Ireland, the commerce and prosperity of this kingdom have eminently increased, and that we can attribute this blessing under Providence to the wisdom of the Irish Parliament." In 1785, three years after the Irish Parliament was established, the exports to England of Irish manufacture and produce amounted annually to two and a half million pounds sterling; whilst the manufactured goods bought of England did not exceed one million pounds, thus affording to Ireland a net gain of one and a half million pounds.

Twelve years later, or three years before the "Union" five and a half million pounds' worth of Irish manufacture and cattle were shipped to England; whilst Ireland only purchased of England to the amount of two millions, leaving a gain to Ireland of three and a half million pounds per annum. The cattle traffic and manufactures of every kind have been monopolized by England. This desperate condition of the Irish nation gave rise to the Volunteer movement of 1778. Goaded by oppressive laws and legislative tyranny, the people took advantage of the defenceless state of the Irish coast, and the numerous threats of foreign invasion that then prevailed throughout Ireland and the Continent. In a short time, the Irish Volunteer army amounted to 90,000 men.* They represented to the government their grievances, and on one occasion, the Volunteer army appeared drawn out in battle array on the streets of Dublin, with cannon and musketry. On the mouths of the cannons, which were pointed towards the House of Parliament, (now the Bank of Ireland) labels bearing the inscription "Free trade or ———." A resolution in compliance with this demand was unanimously voted by the House, there being only one dissenting vote, that of Sir R. Heron, Chief Secretary for Ireland. This concession was virtually a repeal of Poyning's Act. But when England arose out of her international difficulties, she immediately ignored its provisions and nullified the beneficial results that would follow this bold demand for legislative independence.

English capitalists, jealous of the natural resources of the country, defeated all efforts of the Irish people to revive their dying industries. Hence, Ireland has been, and must be, until she obtains a native Parliament, dependent.

* Lord Char'emont co mmanded 60,000 Volunteers.

CHAPTER XIV.

DEPRESSION OF IRISH TRADE, Etc.

IN the absence of foreign trade and commerce, it is regrettable that domestic trades and professions are not encouraged by remunerative wages. At present, a carpenter, tailor, shoe-maker, painter or blacksmith, can seldom earn more than 4 shillings ($1.00) a day, whilst constant employment is by no means secure; the wages of common laborers who are constantly employed, ordinarily, do not exceed 1s. 6d. (less than 40 cents) per diem. A school teacher, a grocery, or dry-goods-clerk, a book-keeper, a telegraph operator, averages an annual salary of £60 ($300). Girls receive still less wages. Young and handsome bar-maids, (no others need apply) shop-girls, milliners, dress-makers and cooks seldom earn more than £10 a year, with board; restaurant waiters and house girls average £5 a year with "tips" (voluntary perquisites). In Dublin, Cork and Limerick the income of a barber may be estimated from his moderate charge of 3d. (6 cents) for shaving, and 6d. (12 cents) for hair-cutting or shampooning. Barbers who charge double these rates are patronized only by the aristocracy. Liquor-dealers, butchers and medical doctors appear to be the most prosperous class; the latter, for a single visit, require a pound ($5.00), a charge which, if the people were dependent on their service, appears to be extortionate.

In order that the reader may form an idea of "living" in Ireland, (1889) a glance over the following tabulated list may be interesting:

	£ s. d.	
First-class hotels charge transient boarders an average of..........(per week)	3. 0. 0	($15.00)
Second-class................... "	1.10. 0	(7.50)
Boarding Houses............... "	0.12. 0	(3.00)
Tea, per pound, averages...............	0. 2. 6	(0.50)
Coffee (seldom used) averages...........	0. 1. 6	(0.36)
Sugar, per pound, "	0. 0. 4	(0.08)
Beef. " "	0. 0. 8	(0.16)
Mutton, " "	0. 0. 8	(0.16)
Bacon, " "	0. 0. 6	(0.12)
Butter, " "	0. 1. 2	(0.28)
Wheat, per stone, "	0. 1. 3	(0.31)
Oats, " "	0. 0. 9	(0.18)
Barley, " "	0. 1. 0	(0.24)
Potatoes, " (14 lbs.) averages......	0. 0. 4	(0.08)
Coal, per ton, (2,240 lbs.) "	1. 5. 0	(6.25)
Railway travel, per mile, 1st class........	0. 0. 2½	(0.04½)
" " " 2nd class........	0. 0. 1½	(0.03)
" " " 3rd class (board seats)...........................	0. 0. 1	(0.02)
Jarvey cars, within corporate limits, per hour, in Dublin 6d., elsewhere, generally.............................	0. 1. 6	(0.36)

As the prices of live cattle, such as horses, cows and sheep fluctuate according to the demand at every fair and market, it would be impossible to furnish a tabulated list of their saleable value; however, at present, stock can be purchased in Ireland at prices similar to those of this country.

There are but three (Nationalist) daily papers worthy of notice in Ireland: the Dublin "Freeman," the Cork "Herald" and Cork "Examiner." In Limerick, there is no daily, but two bi-weeklies, "The Munster News," and "Reporter" which, indeed, are puny specimens of journalism.

Only two cities of Ireland, Dublin and Belfast, have horse cars (tram cars) or paid Fire Companies.

As it might naturally be expected, the best salaried employees in Ireland are government officials. Excise and custom-house officers, coast guards and clerks of the Bank of Ireland receive a salary amounting from 150 to 350 pounds a year. Under the government, however, no officials appear to have such a lucrative and lazy livelihood as the Royal Irish Constablery. They are all well clad, well fed and well domiciled. Nevertheless, as we have already insinuated, they are very unpopular with the citizens and peasantry. While in Germany, France, America and other countries, policemen are respected in their capacity of guardians of "Law and Order;" in Ireland, they are shunted from every popular assemblage. A patriotic Irish girl would rather marry a *spalpeen* than exchange her name for that of the most polished peeler in Her Majesty's service.

Although, in the preceding pages, we had no occasion to furnish instances wherein the British government

---

NOTE. Lest the foregoing comments should contribute to cast undeserved obloquy on the entire police force, we would remind the reader that, as there is no rule that does not admit an exception, so amongst the Irish constablery, are men deserving the good-will and frequently the esteem of their neighbors; consequently, women marrying such men, if they fail to elevate, do not always degrade their caste.

fostered or favored the civil or commercial progress of the Irish nation, still, it would be unfair to ignore the fact that several reformatory measures have been sanctioned since the passage of the "Union Act" (1801).

The first and greatest was the ratification of O'Connell's Emancipation Act of 1826. Before the passage of this Act, Catholics were almost entirely disfranchised; they were not entitled to sit in either House of Parliament; they were excluded from all Universities, from the Bar, the Army, the Navy and civil franchise. Catholics were not permitted to possess swords or fire-arms; to buy or inherit lands from Protestants. A Catholic was not allowed to possess a horse worth more than five pounds; to bequeath property; to act as guardian, or to open or conduct a school. Priests solemnizing marriage between Catholics and Protestants, became liable to the penalty of death; whilst apostate Priests who joined the English church were pensioned for life. Marriages between Catholics and Protestants were declared null and void; whilst no Protestant woman, worth more than £500 could marry a Catholic without forfeiting her estate; Catholic parents were forbidden to send their children to Continental as well as to Irish Catholic schools.

Although many of these odious, (perhaps we might venture to call them barbarous) laws were not enforced after the "Union," still, their ultimate repeal must be attributed to the indefatigable efforts of the LIBERATOR.

The next beneficial law enacted in favor of Ireland was Gladstone's Disestablishment Act of 1869, which exonerated the people from the maintenance of churches and ministers of Anglican profession. The third ameliorative statute was Gladstone's Compensation Act, regulating rentals, and compensating for agrarian improvements (1870-'81). The Acts of '85 and '87, although practically deficient, were also theoretically praiseworthy, as we shall endeavor to show in a subsequent chapter. The British government has also done much for education in Ireland. To assert the fact that the Irish school system is the best in Europe, and that in no other country of the Continent is education more liberal, and universally disseminated, will surprise many of our American readers.

Mr. Chambers, in his "Information for the People," does not hesitate to aver that the Irish *masses* are far better educated than the English or Scotch.

It must also be acknowledged that there are no government statutes to mar the maintenance and progress of religion in Ireland at the present day.

If we take churches and schools as a criterion of domestic prosperity, the aspect of the nation would appear most satisfactory. But while these advantages ought to be duly appreciated, we must not forget that abstract education, tempered by religion, will not provide man with food and raiment.

While the British government fosters education, and never interferes with the practice or profession of religion, by some anomalous oversight or subtle industry, it fails to bestow government positions on Irish Catholic scholars; an English churchman or a Scotch Presbyterian is invariably preferred to an Irish applicant. We are unprepared to decide whether it is malevolence o benevolence that induces the British government to supply poor "Paddy" with a competence of religion, education and potatoes, whilst she grudgingly withholds the precious products of the farm and the orchard.

Irish boys and girls, when well educated, naturally become disgusted with their surroundings; they prefer to EMIGRATE, (just what the land-gentry desire) meanwhile, religion teaches them submission to Law and abstinence from crime.

Indeed, it has been frequently insinuated that if the Irish professed any other creed but Catholicity, they would have long since wrested themselves from the jaws of the British Lion. But it is a unique and a glorious record that the Irish people, although permitting themselves to be robbed of patrimony, still clung to the ancient faith.

Concluding this chapter, we consider it opportune to re-assert that ever since Ireland was linked to her stronger sister, England, so called "Law and Order" have been but empty names in the administration of civil and commercial justice.

CHAPTER XV.

FURTHER EFFECTS OF THE "UNION."

WHILE England, France, Germany, Belgium and other countries name the principal streets of their chief cities after illustrious men or historic houses, the Irish chieftains and their noble deeds are completely ignored in their own country.

Scotland commemorates in bronze and marble her Wallace; Poland, her Kosciusko; England, her Wellington; America, her Washington. But in Ireland, the most costly and artistic* monuments are shafts, urns or human figures commemorative of hostile Englishmen, obsolete scions of Royalty, or officers of the British Army or Navy. In Dublin, (the Metropolis) the chief thoroughfares are named after such elsewhere forgotten English families as Sackville, Marleborough, Dorset, Essex, Harcourt. Passing over Carlisle and King's bridges, we come to Trinity College (where Catholics were spurned) and the Bank of Ireland, once the Irish House of Parliament; Nelson's pillar stands aloft, overlooking aristocratic Nassau, Dawson and Regent streets and Merrion square.

In Limerick, the city of the "Violated Treaty," whilst the smallest street (about 200 feet long) is named after the Hero of Limerick, "Sarsfield," the two leading thoroughfares are called after two of the most ruthless royal tyrants that ever oppressed Ireland, George and William streets (George III and William IV). Here also we see erected (over Wellesley bridge) on a marble pedestal, a gigantic bronze statue of a Lord Fitzgibbon (a Ballaclava warrior); on either side of the monument are two huge cannons imported all the way from Russia; here also by a strange, if not a ludicrous coincidence, we find adjacent *Cecil* and *Roche* streets. (At present, Cecil Roche is the most hated "Removable" in Ireland). The two chief harbors of Ireland are called Kingston and Queenstown. Hospitals, Colleges and Theatres are invariably named after Royalty. "The George," "The Queen's," "The Prince of Wales," "The Imperial," "The King's Arms," "Cruise's Royal," and a thousand other royal etceteras are favorite names of hotels in Ireland. Many business houses and public institutions are called after men who cared no more for Irishmen than a blood-hound does for a fox or a fawn. Rack-rent gentry who caused emigration, have acted even worse than blood-hounds, for *they* leave bones behind. No streets, hotels, bridges or colleges worthy of notice are named after the great Celtic houses "The O'Neill's," "The O'Briens;" nor after the great Norman lines "The Fitzgeralds" and "Butlers." In Dublin, not a single street is named after Swift, Goldsmith, Curran, Burke, Plunket, Wadding or Sarsfield.

Lest we should be answered in retort, we admit that in the United States, we have not only streets, but various cities named after Presidents* and other dis-

---

* Washington is the seat of the Government; while Quincy, Madison, Jefferson, Lincoln, etc., are common city names in the United States.

tinguished statesmen and warriors. But these men, as a general occurrence, lived and fought in the country; whereas, in Ireland, a plurality of those "commemorated" were positively hostile to the Nation and the best interests of the Nation, whilst many of them never resided in the country or saw it except from the deck of a sailing vessel.

Protestant England may well worship her native Heroes and Heroines; but Catholic Ireland, having a galaxy of her own distinguished sons and daughters, should not be coerced to honor the progeny of her sister kingdoms, especially, when we consider that their filial intercourse was not always friendly.

ARGUMENTS THAT APPEAR TO MILITATE AGAINST THE ESTABLISHMENT OF A NATIVE PARLIAMENT IN IRELAND.

1. *A sparse population.*

Canada had a smaller population than the smallest province of Ireland before it obtained Home-Government, whilst the inhabitants who demanded it were declared rebellious.

Belgium, where the farmer owns the soil he cultivates, and where all his improvements become a legacy for his children and posterity, is a smaller country than Ireland; it escaped from the grasp of Holland, a larger and more powerful country, and is now free.

Norway is a smaller country; yet here, the peasant is prosperous and independent; he owns the soil he tills and has a voice in making his country's laws.*

---

* Bulgaria, separating from Turkey, might also be cited.

2. It has been alleged that England and Ireland should not be socially separated since they are so geographically adjacent. Why not? England is nearer to France, which is a larger and richer country, yet they are two distinct nations.

Portugal might be claimed by Spain; Belgium by France; Turkey by Russia, for greater reasons, since they are physically contiguous. In his plea for "Repeal of the Union," O'Connell asserted that Ireland was fit for legislative independence in position, population and natural advantages. He maintained that five independent kingdoms of Europe possessed less territory and people, while her situation on the Atlantic, between the old and the new world, destined her to be the entrepôt of both, had not the wrathful jealousy of England rendered her natural advantages nugatory. Instead of the present scant population (4,500,000) Ireland is capable of supporting 20,000,000 people.

"No country of Europe," says a great writer, "can compare with Ireland in the exquisite variety of its scenery, in the loveliness of its green fields, in the magnificence of its lofty mountains, and in the multitude of its ever-flowing streams." Another writer apostrophizes: "We view with amazement an island, favored with all the conditions of great commerce, as bare of commerce as if it lay on some bye-way of the world which enterprise has not yet reached; the noble quays of the Liffey would rival the Lung d'Arno, if Dublin were the seat of national government, at present, only holding a few coal-barges and fruit boats."*

Although the lordly mansions and turretted castles

---

* Sir Gavan Duffy.

that overhang the banks of the Rhine in Europe, and the large and prosperous cities that indent the Hudson in America, excel anything that art or architecture has done for the rivers Shannon and Blackwater (called the Irish Rhine); yet the romantic villas, enclosed by fragrant hedges of hawthorn, lilac and woodbine, and the ivy-crowned ruins that nestle in the miniature forests that overshadow the banks of these two lovely streams, are incomparably more charming. The bold cliffs and fantastic scenery that surround Kilkee, (an Irish bathing resort) outrival all that nature has done for the bay of Newport, although the wealth of Bellevue avenue, in the latter city, would be more than sufficient to purchase the entire county Clare in Ireland.

3. It has been advanced in objection, that the Irish have always been a fickle and divided people; that ancient History records the lives of native Kings and Chieftains continually at war, and the country itself divided into hostile Septs, Clans, etc., and are consequently incapable of self-government.

A majority of Ireland's national disunions might be traced to English perfidy. From the day the Saxon first set his foot upon Irish soil, he endeavored to disseminate jealousies and hatred amongst the natives. It was only by such chicanery that he could expect to live and prosper in the country; hence, traitors and informers were always encouraged and rewarded, even the extant Tory government regards such national apostates as Cary, Le Caron, and Pigott, valuable promoters of its Irish policy.

But overlooking past disunions, which, perhaps time and circumstances warranted, the present inhabitants of Ireland, with whom the government must negotiate, are almost unanimous in their demand for self-government.

4. The Orangemen of Ulster and elsewhere insist on maintenance of the "Union," even at the risk of armed revolt; the Irish gentry and Protestants are naturally opposed to Home Rule, fearing Catholic ascendency would persecute, and eventually force them to leave the country. Although such arguments have been frequently flaunted by Col. Saunderson and other Orange bigots, they are, however, almost unworthy of notice.

In the first place, Orangemen of Ulster and elsewhere in Ireland do not aggregate a seventh part the entire population. The threat of war then, is a ridiculous bluff. Secondly, Catholics in Ireland have never persecuted their Protestant brethren. On the contrary, in the past as well as at present, they have placed national confidence in men of that profession. Lord Charlemont (who commanded the Irish Volunteers), Grattan, Robert Emmet, Lord Ed. Fitzgerald, James Napper Tandy, Flood, Dean Swift, Dr. Lucas, Molyneux—later on, John Mitchell and Isaac Butt, (the father of Home Rule) were all Protestants.

The Protestant clergymen, William Jackson, William Porter, Warwick, and Stevelley, and the Catholic Priests, Fathers Philip Roche, John and Michael Murphy, Kearns, Prendegrast and Quigley, worshiping at different shrines, sacrificed their lives upon the same altar of freedom.

NOTE. Dr. Madden states that the organizing leaders of the movements of '98 and '48 included Protestants and Catholics; the former being to the latter in the proportion of four to one.

In addition to the above mentioned names, the following prominent advocates of Irish autonomy were Protestants: Curran, Burke,

At present, the chief promoters of Home Rule, Charles Stewart Parnell, Hon. Wm. E. Gladstone, Earl Spencer, Lord Roseberry, Lord Aberdeen, John Morley, Sir Vernon Harcourt, even the late Mayor elect of Dublin (Winstanley), are of Protestant persuasion.

Thomas Adis Emmet, William and Samuel Orr, Hamilton Rowan, Mathew Keugh, Thos. Russell and Revs. W. Steele, Dickson, Butler and Ferguson.

5*

CHAPTER XVI.

WHAT IRISHMEN HAVE DONE FOR ANCIENT AND MODERN CIVILIZATION.

THAT the people of Ireland should be incapable of self-government, appears to be an insolvable paradox when we consider that in other countries, Irishmen have held the first positions in Church and State; whilst many of them were the leading pioneers of liberty and civilization.

Long before the blood-thirsty Danes and grasping Normans landed upon the coasts of Ireland, the nation stood at the head of European civilization. As the morning star occupies a conspicuous place in the Heavens, so does Ireland in the galaxy of great nations. As early as the fifth century, Greek and Roman literature, sacred art and philosophy were common studies, not only of the monasteries, but of the undisciplined laity.

To narrate proud facts of ancient Irish history, we need not unearth the mummies of the Tuatha de Danann warriors or disturb the ashes of the 118 Kings of the Milesian race whom ancient Celtic chronicles (as reliable as the rhapsodies of Homer or Virgil) have immortalized. To adorn fair Erin's saintly brow with a chaplet of precious gems, we need not go back to the halcyon days of Queen Mab, Oisin and Conar Mac Messa, when it was impossible to discriminate between the dusk of fable and the dawn of authentic history. We shall relate a few facts that are confirmed by evidence as sacred as can corroborate human records.

St. David, born of an Irish mother, was the Apostle of Wales; St. Columbkille, the glory of Scotland; St. Killian, the Apostle of Franconia; St. Nidon, the patron of Northumberland, were Irishmen. If France gave to Ireland St. Patrick, Ireland, in later years, repaid her a hundred fold. In the annals of the Four Masters,* we read that the Emperor Charlemagne appointed as rector of the universities of Paris and Pavia, Johannes Scotus Erigena (an Irishman) who afterwards became tutor of King Alfred the Great. Montalambert, in his "Monks of the West," gives a glowing account of the culture of Irish monasteries. A synod at Kells, A. D. 1152, under the papal legate, Paparo, incorporated the Irish schools into the ecclesiastical system of Rome.

An able German American writer, (Rev. Wm. Stang, D. D.) has recently recorded in book form "Germany's *Debt* to Ireland," which acknowledges that a certain St. Benedict (an Irish Saint), while sojourning in Rome was elected Pope, but declined the proferred dignity, and that Virgilius, who taught the sphericity of the earth long before Copernicus or Kepler, was sent from Ireland to Germany as Bishop of Saltzburg. Indeed, there is not a civilized country of Europe that does not owe a debt of gratitude to Ireland.

It is a fact recorded in revised Catholic History that

---

* Michael O'Clerigh, a Franciscan friar, was the Author of the "Annals."

in Italy, the patron Saints of thirteen countries were Irishmen; Belgium venerates 50; Scotland, 76; England, 44; France, 47; Iceland, 9, and Germany, 102.

The State as well as the Church is indebted to Irish heads and hands. When Sarsfield surrendered Limerick to King William of Orange, 1691, thousands of Irish soldiers who had fought with King James, disgusted with his pusillanimity and scorning to serve under the Hanovarian flag, joined the banners of France and Spain, and by their genius and bravery emblazoned their names on the historic page of both countries. It was Irishmen who decided the fortune of the day at Fontenoy, and extorted from George II that memorable exclamation "Cursed be the laws that have deprived me of such subjects."

> "Mother of soldiers in the cause of Spain
> The Moors in Oran's trench by them were slain;
> For full one hundred years their fatal steel
> Has charged beside the lances of Castile
> And Spain, of honor jealous, gave them place
> Before her native sons in glory's race."

"When our forefathers threw off the British yoke," says Wm. Mathews, LL.D., (a Protestant American writer) "the Irish formed a sixth part of the whole population, and one-fourth of all the commissioned officers in the army and navy were of Irish descent. The first General killed in battle, the first artillery officer appointed, the first commodore commissioned, the first victor to whom the British flag was struck at sea, and the first officer who surprised a fort by land, were Irishmen." Lord Mountjoy once declared before the British House of Parliament, "You have lost America through the Irish." As they fought for the independence of the

United States, so they fought and helped to maintain the independence of South America. The footsteps of the Celt can be traced from the forests of Maine to the farthest shadows of the Andes.

Ireland gave Wellington and Wolsey to England; O'Donnell* to Spain; McMahon to France; O'Higgins** and Brown† to South America; and Andrew Jackson,†† Carroll, Calhoun,‡ Stewart and Barry (the father of the U. S. Navy) to the United States. Whilst there is a respectable library extant, the following names will never be ignored: Moore, Swift, Goldsmith, Burke, Lever, Lover, Curran, Carleton, Griffin and O'Connell. At present, many of the highest offices in the government of Australia, Canada, and the United States, as also the most honorable municipal positions are entrusted to Irishmen.‡‡

Considering that in the United States and Canada, there are hundreds of thousands of Catholics of all civilized nationalities, Ireland may well feel proud of the

* O'Donnell (L. O'Donel Span.) was Duke of Tetuan and Marshal of Spain.

** Ambrose O'Higgins (called the great Viceroy of Chili) was born in Co. Meath, and appointed Viceroy of Chili in 1788.

† Admiral Brown was born in Co. Mayo in 1777; he was appointed Commodore of the Chilian Navy in 1814.

†† Andrew Jackson's father emigrated from Co. Donegal in 1733.

‡ Calhoun's parents emigrated from Carrickfergus, Co. Antrim in 1765.

‡‡ The late Commander in Chief of the United States Army, Gen. Phil. Sheridan, was an Irishman. Ex-Mayors Grace of New York and O'Brien of Boston, and the acting Mayor of New York (Grant) are Irishmen and Catholics.

fact that of the fourteen Archbishops* of the United States (in '89), ten, including the Cardinal, are Irish or of Irish descent; of the seven Archbishops of Canada and the West Indies, four are natives of Ireland; of the seventy-seven Bishops who form the American Episcopate, forty-two are Irish or of Irish descent.

When we thus see the church and those wise and great governments conferring on Irishmen the highest offices in their gift, we may conclude without prejudice, that England fails to award their deserts to her so-called sister's children across the Channel.

* His Eminence, Cardinal Gibbons (Baltimore); their Graces, Archbishops Corrigan (New York), Ryan (Philadelphia), Williams (Boston), Feehan (Chicago), Kendrick (St. Louis), Elder (Cincinnati), Grace (St. Paul), Ireland (St. Paul), Riordan (San Francisco). Canada:—Archbishops Cleary (Kingston), O'Brien (Halifax), Walsh (Toronto), Flood (West Indies).

NOTE. Not wishing to detract from the credit due Christopher Columbus for his discoveries, the following records are worthy of serious consideration:—

In the Bibliotheque Nationale, Paris, there are thirteen different manuscripts of the 8th and 9th centuries, showing that St. Brendin, Abbot of Clonfert, Ireland, made the first voyage to the western coast about the year 515. Other manuscripts of similar import are in the British Museum, the Bodleian library at Oxford, and the library at Nuremberg. It is possible that Columbus got the first ideas for his voyage from these manuscripts.

CHAPTER XVII.

THE LAND ACTS OF 1870, '81, '85, AND '87; THE TENANTS DEFENCE ASSOCIATION, AND THE IRISH POLITICAL PLATFORM.

EXCEPT the Act of 1871, which existed nine years prior to the establishment of the Land League, the three subsequent land Acts and indeed, every ameliorative measure recently sanctioned by the British government, owe their existence to the Land League or national agitation and the Plan of Campaign. No attempts to solve the agrarian question in past years have afforded so much satisfaction as the reluctant legislative efforts that have been made during the past twenty years. Although we persistently maintain that the land trouble is not sole cause of Ireland's discontent, still it must be avowed that the recent land acts are ameliorative and praiseworthy.

The Act of 1870 gave the tenant a certain amount of security against the capricious despotism of the landlord, at whose mercy he had heretofore always been; it further provided compensation for improvements. Prior to this Act, all improvements made by the tenant were the landlord's property. This Act transferred their ownership to the tenant who, in case of eviction, could file a claim against the landlord for their value.

The Act of '81 improved on the Act of 1870, by giving the tenant absolute security of tenure. It established an (*alleged*) independent tribunal to fix fair rent. It legalized the tenant's interest in his holding, and made it salable in the open market to the highest bidder. It was assuredly an ameliorative step towards allaying land grievances. Under this, and the Act of '87, some 314,000 tenancies have been adjudicated. The Act of '85, called the "Ashbourne Act," was first conceived by Mr. Bright in 1869. Lord Ashbourne introduced and carried a measure placing the sum of £5,000,000 at the disposal of those Irish tenants who desired to purchase the fee-simple of their holdings, provided the landlords were willing to sell. (Here, we would parenthetically remark, that few landlords were disposed to sell except on terms that savored extortion). The Act provided for the re-payment of principal and interest by the payment of forty-nine annual instalments, after which time the occupier became the owner of the land. The Act of '87 established a Royal Commission for the purpose of adjusting agrarian difficulties. It opened the doors of the Court to a majority of leaseholders who were, heretofore, excluded from the benefits of the previous Acts. It also subjected the rents judicially fixed in 1881–'85 to revision. Finally, it authorized the tenant, when summoned for non-payment of rent, to show if it were impossible for him to pay the rent demanded. If he could do this, the county court Judge was authorized to stay eviction, and also to fix a fair rent, and was empowered to spread the arrears over any period he thought fit. This would be an excellent piece of legislation were it not a fact that the Land Commissioners and county court Judges are naturally biased towards the other side, most of them being landlords themselves. It practically turned out similar to the fable of the Wolf and the Lamb; the wolf could dictate terms to the lamb; whilst lambs, at the mercy of wolves, need expect no quarter. Lord Londonderry, (the Viceroy) who appointed the Commissioners, was himself an inflexible landlord, feared and hated by a plurality of his Irish tenantry. Moreover, since arrears were left untouched, a free gift of the land to the tenant would not improve his condition whilst this mill-stone of rack-rent arrears hung about his neck. Hence, landlords in every part of Ireland have taken advantage of this culpable flaw in the Act, and have, and are still evicting tenants by the hundred for the non-payment of impossible arrears. The conditional Arrears' Act of 1872 did not benefit five out of every hundred tenants who were in arrears. Mr. Parnell's Bill of '88, purporting to relieve the tenants thus complicated, was ignobly defeated by the Tory government. Indeed, the Irish tenantry may justly regard the House of Peers, a house of implacable landlords. Recently, (Dec. 1889) another land-purchase

N. B. A clause in the land Act of '85 provided that a laborer, securing the approval of a majority of the Poor Law Guardians of the district, could have a homestead built him at the expense of the government. To re-imburse this loan, the laborer was required to pay a small sum every week (generally six pence) for a certain number of years, after whose expiration he became the absolute owner. The house stood on a quarter-acre ground lot, taken from the lands of some neighboring farmer. These cottages, built of plastered stone and covered with slate, and generally consisting of two rooms and a kitchen, were commodious and comfortable habitations. At present such cottages are being erected within an average radius of three miles throughout the entire country. They are certainly a great improvement compared with the old thatched mud cabins.

scheme has been devised and sanctioned by Lords Salisbury, Ashbourne and Mr. Balfour, but this, as the former, we do not hesitate to predict, will prove equally abortive.

THE NEW TENANTS' DEFENCE ASSOCIATION.
(1889-'90).

Owing to a recent hostile combination of landlords, and especially to a threat of a Cork and Tipperary landlord, (Mr. Smith-Barry)* averring his resolve to introduce colonies of English and Scotch settlers to occupy the lands of tenants evicted from the Ponsonby estate, (a great part of the Brooke estate has been already thus planted) the Irish leaders, headed by Mr. Parnell, have instituted a counter-combination, called the "Tenants' Defence Association," which threatens to become a formidable obstacle to the wanton rapacity of the rack-renting gentry.

This Association possesses decided advantage over the National League and the Plan of Campaign in as much as its tactics (unlike those of the former, proscribed by civil law, and the latter by civil and ecclesiastical laws) are in accordance with the extant laws of the Church and State.

The members of this Association can assemble when and where they please, and are free to coöperate in their self-defensive policy without becoming outlaws in the

* Up to February, 1890, over a hundred shopkeepers, including some 1100 souls have been evicted from their business stores in the town of Tipperary, by the landlord Smith-Barry. The evicted tenants have selected other sites and are actively employed building NEW to replace OLD TIPPERARY. Two thousand tenants have been evicted from the Ponsonby estate.

eyes of the government. Although its establishment is of recent date (Sept. '89) it has branches flourishing in every part of the country.*

That the programme of this Association harmonizes with the voice of the Catholic Church may be assumed from the fact that it has been formally approved by the four Archbishops, and the entire Episcopate of Ireland, including the heretofore recalcitrant nationalist, Dr. O'Dwyer, Bishop of Limerick.

Irishmen in America will be especially pleased to know that their Graces, the four Archbishops of Ireland, (Walsh, Loague, Croke and MacEvilly) sent not only encouraging letters, but monetary subscriptions to the promoters of the new League. We presume the following extract letter from the gifted pen of the Archbishop of Tuam will be read with pleasure:

ST. JARLATH'S, TUAM, Dec. 8, 1889.

DEAR FATHER DOOLEY:—I received in due course your letter written on behalf of the "Tenants' Defence Association."

In presence of a Landlord Syndicate, professedly organized to perpetuate the old state of injustice and abject serfdom, under which the tenants of this country have been so long suffering, a powerful and opulent confederacy, threatening what may be regarded as nothing short of a war of extermination to be carried on, not simultaneously, but piecemeal, against the bravest and most determined, it would be strange, if, in the face of such a powerful confederacy, the tenants of Ireland did not, on their part, combine peaceably and legally, as one man, in self-defence, while their very existence in the land of their birth is at stake.

For my own part, I could not but reproach myself with a gross dereliction of duty if I failed to sanction or give my humble support to any association, conducted within the limits of law, having for its

* Up to February 1, 1890, the funds of the Association amounted to £45,800.

object to save from utter extirpation and the horrors of enforced emigration with all its well-known attendant evils, both moral and physical, the remnant of our population day by day on the decrease.

I send annexed £10 as a practical expression of my approval.

I remain,
Very faithfully yours,
✠ John MacEvilly,
Archbishop of Tuam.

IRISH PLATFORM.

John Mitchell, in his "Letters to small farmers of Ireland," furnished an apposite precedent for the present Irish policy. Mitchell mentioned a certain farmer named Boland, who, although cultivating twenty acres of land, was, with his family, found dead in their beds, of starvation. "Now," said he, "what became of poor Boland's twenty acres of crop? A part of it went to Gibraltar to victual the garrison, part went to Spain to pay for the landlord's wine, part to London to pay the interest of his honor's mortgage to the Jews. The English ate some of it, the Chinese had their share, but none was left for poor Boland.

The plain remedy for all this is to reverse the order of payment; to take and keep out of the crops you raise, your own subsistence, and that of your families and laborers, first. . . "If it needs all your crop to keep you alive, you will be justified in refusing payment of any rent, tribute, rate or taxes whatever. To do this effectually, you must combine with your neighbors; you must form voluntary defence associations, in order to be able to repel your oppressors."

Toward the conclusion of the same letter Mitchell said, "But I am told it is in vain to speak thus to you;

that the Peace policy of O'Connell is dearer to you than life and honor; that some of your clergy exhort you rather to die than violate what the English call 'Law.' Then *die*--die in your patience and perseverance; but be well assured of this—that the Priest or person who bids you perish amidst your own golden harvests, preaches the gospel of tyranny, insults manhood and common sense, and bears false witness against religion, and blasphemes the Providence of God."

Perhaps it would be impossible to furnish more authentic information on the present political movement than to quote Mr. Parnell's explanation of the Home Rule movement, recently addressed to a meeting in Nottingham (Dec. 17, '89). "The object of the Home Rule movement," he said, "was to regenerate Ireland, especially with regard to her industrial condition." Mr. Parnell contended that manufactures should be developed to such an extent as to take the strain off the land, and enable the people to look to other avocations besides farming for gaining a livelihood; he opposed the idea that Ireland should have England promote her industries. "Irishmen themselves must promote Irish industries by building harbors, clearing out channels, and reclaiming waste lands, not at the expense of the English, but of the Irish exchequer, or best of all, through the efforts of local and individual enterprise, and with private capital."

The political platform endorsed by Mr. Parnell, Gladstone and the Irish Representatives does not require complete separation from England. It simply embodies the demand for a Home Parliament—a relation such as Canada bears to England, or each State to the United States. The Imperial Court of England was to have the same power as the Supreme Court of the United States in the definition of a national question.

Mr. Michael Davitt in a speech (Jan. 26, '81) said, "Our League does not desire to intimidate any one who disagrees with us; while we condemn coercion, we must not be guilty of coercion." The theories of the Land League by no means harmonize with the teachings of those who deny private property or ownership. While aiming at the establishment of a peasant proprietorship, they allow rent for the landlord, profit for the farmer, wages for the laborer; and out of this rent, profit and wages, professionals shall get fees, shopkeepers custom, artisans employment; and that from the united profits of all these incomes, manufactures and commerce should flourish.

They contend that it was neither just nor expedient that the Parliament of Westminster composed of but one hundred and three Irish members against more than five hundred Scotch, Welsh and English members, should pass laws affecting Ireland against the will of the majority of the Irish Representatives, whilst the Executive for England was not the Irish Executive, but the avowed enemy of the people.

The following extract from a speech of Mr. John Redmond, M. P., delivered before the Chicago convention, held in 1886, further elucidates Ireland's political policy:

"The principle embodied in the Irish movement of to-day is just the same principle which was the soul of every Irish movement for the past seven centuries; the principle of rebellion against the rule of strangers; the principle which Owen Rowe O'Neill vindicated, which animated Tone and Fitzgerald, and for which Emmet sacrificed a stainless life. Let no man desecrate that principle by giving it the ignoble name of hatred to England. Race-hatred is at best, but an unreasoning passion. I, for one, believe in the brotherhood of nations; and bitter as the memory is of past wrongs, and present injustice inflicted on our people by our alien rulers, I assert the principle underlying our movement is not the principle of revenge for the past, but of justice for the future. We believe it is possible to bring about a settlement honorable to England and Ireland alike, whereby the wrongs and miseries of the past may be sorgotten, the chapter of English wrongs and Irish refistance may be closed, and there may be future freedom and amity between the two nations"

That the day may soon arrive when such an amicable settlement shall be consummated, should be the prayer of every true Irishman throughout the earth.

APPENDIX.

ROMAN CATHOLIC CHURCH, (1881).

The Roman Catholic Church in Ireland is governed by four Archbishops, twenty-three Bishops and two mitred Abbots. In Ireland, there are 3,047 Priests (1,010 P. Ps., 1,719 C. Cs., and 318 Regulars); 1,089 Churches, 98 Monasteries, and 288 Convents.

RELIGIONS.

Catholics	4,127,347
Episcopalians	635,670
Presbyterians	385,583
Methodists	47,669
Baptists	4,957
All other denominations about	40,000
Total population in 1881	5,241,226
In 1888	4,777,534
In 1890, about	4,500,000

PARLIAMENT.

The present British Parliament (elected July, 1886), is composed of two Houses, the House of Lords and the House of Commons, (London). The House of Lords consists of 2 Princes of the blood, 2 Archbishops, 24 Bishops, 282 Barons, 16 Scotch Peers, elected for each Parliament and 28 Irish Peers elected for life.

The House of Commons is composed of 670 members, of whom 465 represent England; 30, Wales; 72, Scotland; 103, Ireland. Of the Irish members, 94 are Home Rulers.

NAMES OF IRISH NATIONALIST MEMBERS OF PARLIAMENT WITH THEIR CONSTITUENCIES. (1890).

Antrim,
J. H. MacKelvey.
Armagh,
J. Williamson,
R. Gardner,
A. Blaine.
Belfast,
J. M'Erlean,
T. Sexton.
Carlow,
The O'Gorman Mahon.
Cavan,
J. G. Biggar,
T. O'Hanlon.
Clare,
J. R. Cox,
J. Jordan.
Cork City,
C. S. Parnell,
M. Healy.
Cork County,
J. C. Flynn,
William O'Brien,
Dr. C. Tanner,
W. J. Lane,
J. Gilhooly,
Dr. J. E. Kenny,
J. M. M'Morrow.
Donegal,
J. E. O'Doherty,
P. O'Hea,
A. O'Connor,
J. G. S. MacNeill.
Down,
—— M'Nabb,
J. B. McHugh,

H. McGrath,
M. M'Cartan.
Dublin City,
T. D. Sullivan,
T. Harrington,
Thos. A. Dickson,
W. Murphy,
Hugh Johnson,
E. P. S. Counsel.
Dublin County,
J. J. Clancy,
Sir T. Esmonde.
Fermanagh,
W. H. Redmond,
H. Campbell.
Galway,
J. Pinkerton,
P. J. Foley,
Col. Nolan,
David Sheehy,
M. Harris.
Kerry,
John Stack,
E. Harrington,
D. Kilbride,
J. D. Sheehan.
Kildare,
J. L. Carew,
Jas. Leahy.
Kilkenny,
Thomas Quinn,
E. M. Marum,
P. A. Chance.
King's County,
Dr. J. Fox,
B. C. Molloy.

6

Leitrim,
M. Conway,
L. P. Hayden.
Limerick City,
F. A. O'Keffe.
Limerick County,
W. Abraham,
J. Finucane.
Londonderry,
J. M'Carthy,
T. M. Healy.
Longford,
Dr. Fitzgerald.
Louth,
J. Nolan,
T. P. Gill.
Mayo,
D. Crilly,
J. Deasy,
J. F. X. O'Brien,
John Dillon.
Meath,
Pierce Mahony,
E. Sheil.
Monaghan,
Patrick O'Brien,
Sir J. M'Kenna,
J. H. M'Carthy.
Queen's County.
W. M'Donald,

R. Lalor.
Roscommon.
J. O'Kelly,
Dr. A. Comyns.
Sligo,
P. M'Donald,
E. Leamy, B. L.
Tipperary,
P. J. O'Brien,
Thos. Mayne,
J. O'Connor,
T. J. Condon.
Tyrone,
J. O. Wiley,
M. J. Kenny,
W. J. Reynolds.
Waterford,
Richard Power,
T. J. Power.
Westmeath,
James Tuite,
D. Sullivan.
Wexford,
J. E. Redmond,
S. Barry.
Wicklow,
G. M. Byrne,
W. J. Corbett.

PRINCIPAL OCCUPATIONS OF EMIGRANTS WHO LEFT IRELAND DURING YEARS 1887-1888.

Males.	1888	Males.	1888
Bakers, Confectioners..	167	Masons and Paviors....	120
Blacksmiths...........	118	Mechanics...........	65
Boot and Shoe Makers..	182	Painters, Glaziers,	
Carpenters and Joiners..	432	Plumbers, etc........	138
Clerks & Accountants..	627	Servants............	153
Coopers..............	73	Shopkeepers and Shop	
Farmers..............	1,687	Assistants..........	462
Labourers............	31,952	Tailors..............	192

Females.	1888	Females.	1888
Dressmakers and Milliners............	418	Housekeepers........	2,364
		Seamsters, etc........	2;0
Millworkers..........	35	Servants............	26,500

NUMBER OF EMIGRANTS, NATIVES OF IRELAND.

Year.	Number.	Year.	Number.
1877...............	38,503	1884...............	75,863
1878...............	41,124	1885...............	62,034
1879...............	47,065	1886...............	63,135
1880...............	95,517	1887...............	82,923
1881...............	78,417	1888...............	78,684
1882...............	89,136		
1883...............	108,724	Total, 1851-88.....	3,276,103

Of the 78,684 natives of Ireland who emigrated in 1888, 72,988, or 92.8 per cent. went to the colonies or to foreign countries, and 5,696 or 7.2 per cent. to Great Britain. The United States of America absorbed 66,906, or 85.0 per cent. of the number of native emigrants in 1888, compared with an average of 56,744, or 79.9 per cent. for the four preceding years. The number of emigrants to New Zealand, which fell from 809 in 1884 to 429 in 1885 and to 208 in 1886, rose to 322 in 1887, but decreased to 87 in 1888. Emigration to Canada likewise shows a decrease in 1888 compared with 1887, the numbers being 2,686 as against 3,769. The emigrants to Australia numbered 3,110 in 1888, as against 3,896 in 1887. Of the 66,906 emigrants to the United States in 1888, Munster contributed 22,535; Ulster, 18,706; Connaught, 14,265; Leinster, 11,200.

Perhaps the most striking proof of national decadency is the fact that although the population of Ireland exceeded that of Scotland by 770,000 in '88, the record of births and marriages for Ireland was but 109,557 and 20,060 respectively, against 123,233 births and 25,281 marriages for Scotland; whilst the deaths in Ireland during the same year exceeded those of Scotland by 14,876.

A SYNOPSIS

OF

IRISH SCENERY, MINSTRELSY AND CHARACTER.

Dear to my heart are the scenes of my childhood
  While fond recollection presents them to view,
The orchard, the meadow, the deep-tangled wildwood
  And every loved spot which my infancy knew.

S. WOODWORTH.

PRELUDE.

In view of the fact that those who received their christian or patronymic names in Ireland aggregate one-fifth the entire population of the United States, we presume many of our American readers will be pleased to glance over the subsequent pages, purporting to exhibit the latest views of the country and people. Although apparently promiscuous selections, the author begs to state that a certain limit of order has been observed in their compilation.

We may judge of a nation as of an individual by scanning the features, the voice, the characteristics. Such a method has been adopted in the following treatise:

1. Landscape and scenery, representing the physical features of the nation.
2. Minstrelsy, repeating the voice of the nation.
3. Traits and characteristics, forestalling the culture of the nation.

If we collocate these traits with the political prospects discussed in the foregoing chapters, we shall have a systematic guide to the character of Ireland and the Irish people.

Having sifted all its misgivings, the reader will find the nation furnishes a glorious record. Those lukewarm Irishmen who are loath to identify themselves with "Paddy's land" have no cause to feel ashamed; on the contrary, they have unequivocal reasons to feel proud of their motherland.

And if a cluster of shamrocks or a handful of earth from the "Old

Sod" often affect the tenderest feelings of the Celtic heart, we trust this little volume, "Ireland in '89," will serve as a "reminder" not only to Irishmen who never expect to see again the land of their birth, but also to Americans who, without crossing the "*waters*" can learn so much domestic Irish history   .

AN IRISH LANDSCAPE.*

AS a person peering through a kaleidescope can describe only those objects that are exposed to his inspection, at one time, for equivalent reasons, it would be impossible for a writer to convey, in a brief essay, an adequate notion of the scenery of a country comprising 32,000 square miles of land and water.

A radius of five miles is frequently more than the human eye can encompass within the limits of any horizon in Ireland; moreover, besides the novelty of the seasons, the ever changing variety of mountain, river and woodland, reveals charms chiefly enhanced by their immediate surroundings.

Waiving then, the infeasible task of presenting a general view, we trust the following particular description will prove interesting. We shall especially notice those objects that engross the attention of the three leading senses; the eye, the ear, and the nasal organs.

Sitting on one of the lovely hills that adorn the southern portion of the county of ———, on a sunny April day, the eye beholds a charming panorama. Around us, far and near, we see numerous herds of

---

* The above description notes only the leading objects visible in an area of five square miles. There are ten thousand such landscapes more or less beautiful in other parts of the Island. The physical beauties of the Lakes of Killarney, the Vale of Avoca, Glengariff, Lismore, etc., are far more charming and picturesque.

cattle greedily cropping the fresh green herbage, or ruminating as they indolently lie on the heather; flocks of sheep and lambs gamboling with all the antics innocence and satiety can suggest, and birds of every species and hue feeding their young or procuring material for their prospective nests.

On the western horizon, mantled in gossamery clouds, we see the rugged peaks of the McGillycuddy reeks overlooking the Devil's Punch Bowl and the Gap of Dunloe; and towards the east, the cone-shaped "Keeper Hill" and the "Galty" mountains of Tipperary. At a less remote distance, we discover the spires and lofty steeples of Limerick's far-famed churches glistening in the sunshine, and more conspicuous still, the great tall chimney of the once famous Russell Factory.

Winding its sinuous course through purple, emerald and crimson forests and verdant dales, washing on either side the extremities of Tipperary, Clare, Limerick and Kerry counties, and kissing the while the mossy banks of Bunratty, Tarbert and Kilrush, we see the lordly Shannon bearing on its placid bosom numerous craft, from the frail canoe to the more pretending sloop, schooner and steam yacht. The colossal buttresses of Bunratty's once castellated fortress loom up in the western horizon, whilst almost beneath the shadow of the great M—— mountains, the ivy-covered mural ruins of C——'s and P——'s castles stand out in bold relief before the naked eye.

As we review these charming scenes of passive nature, the shrill whistle of the E—— train rumbling, rattling and belching an interminable streak of steam, forewarns its near approach. It is delightful to watch the butterfly and the honey bee flitting from flower to flower, occasionally burying their tiny heads beneath the velvet petals in their efforts to sip nectar from their dewy bosoms.

Whilst the eye beholds the hills and dales, covered with snow-white carpets of daisies, interspersed with oily buttercups, primroses and daffodils, the nasal organs are not less interested; for the surrounding white and black thorn hedges are variegated with budding lilacs and furze, whose refreshing aroma commingles with the redolence of holly, hazel and woodbine. All budding and blossoming nature announce the advent of the sweetest summer that mortals can enjoy upon this earth. But the feast which rural landscape furnishes to the eye and the nose is not to be compared to the ineffable delights that entrance the ear.

The carols of feathered songsters fill all vacant space with the music of their warbling; whilst the Cuckoo, Thrush and Blackbird are heard only in season, the song of the Lark* and the sweet notes of the Robin are never hushed.

From his isolated nest in the sylvan glade or silent meadow, the Lark soars almost perpendicularly, singing the while, until he is almost lost to sight in the clouds. Here, with out-spread wings, apparently motionless, he carols forth the sweetest and most enchanting lays. Now and then he will descend, singing until he reaches the ground where its nest is usually located. It is said this creature never loses sight of its nest during its lofty flight. This charming little song-bird is scarcely ever silent except during midnight hours, or whilst feeding its young. From the earliest dawn, before the sun ap-

---

* Sometimes called Sky-lark.

pears on the horizon, the creatures shrill notes are heard through hill and vale. The earliest notion of rising in the morning is popularly associated with the first flight of the Lark. During the spring, summer and autumn months, it is impossible to travel anywhere through the woods, mountains or valleys without being within the range of this creature's voice; and not only one, but a chorus of such sweet voices fill the surrounding air with their resonant melody.

But of all the feathered tribe that nestle in the forest or paint in the landscape, there is none entitled to more human sympathy than the Robin, or Red-breast as he is commonly called by the peasantry. This little creature (about the size of an English sparrow) is so familiar with man and domestic animals, that he will not betake to flight, but remain sitting on some pendant bough, warbling his soft notes within a few feet of passers-by. It is amusing to watch the creature flying from tree to tree, as he attempts to keep pace with the traveller and cheer him with the music of his song.

In winter, the Robin becomes bolder; when snow has overspread the earth, he frequently alights on the threshold or window-sill waiting to receive a few crumbs. When other birds are silent through the winter and greater part of spring, the Robin's familiar notes are seldom missed from the leafless hawthorns or naked boughs. Wanton school boys who do not scruple to rob birds' nests, discriminate in favor of the Robin's, deeming it a sacrilege to meddle with its nest or eggs. And this tiny warbler, as though aware of the popular superstition, often builds his capacious domicile on trees and bushes growing but a few feet from the school-room or homestead. In the farm-yard and kitchen-garden the Robin superintends all operations; the carpenter and smithy regard him as a welcome visitor; the laborer, as a friend; the farmer, as a companion who first salutes him in the morning and again greets him as he returns in the evening. His song always inspires joy to the joyful and sympathy with the sorrowful. Although the most domestic of birds, it will not live encaged or confined. The Robin frequents the poorest cabin as well as the proudest villas. His distended crimson breast bespeaks good cheer, whilst his swelling throat never fails to brighten our hopes and soothe our cares.

KILKEE.

"Ille terrarum mihi praeter omnes
   Angulus ridet." (Horace Carm. II, 6).

Kilkee, (church of St. Kee) is a neat little village in county Clare, eight miles from Kilrush, and about forty from Limerick, from whose port a steamer starts every day for Kilrush. The bay of Kilkee is one of the most delightful bathing resorts in Ireland—perhaps, in Europe. It is incomparably superior to Newport, the great American bathing resort. Sheltered by a ledge of rocks that circumvent at least one-third of the entire bay, the attractions of this delightful place are irresistible; whilst the coast is one of the finest in creation. Cliffs do not melt into the ocean, as in other coasts, but they tower perpendicularly from the deep, with a majestic supremacy that proclaim the presidency of the Almighty Architect that placed them there an insuperable barrier between the restless, ever rolling billows of the Atlantic and the mainland. Islands spring from the depths of the sea and are scattered far out from the shore, covered with emerald verdure feeding flocks of sheep and goats. It is a puzzle to ascertain how they are placed upon, or taken from these green oases in which they are fattened for the market, to supply the sweetest mutton in the world. Rocks, apparently piled up by Titan arms boldly shoot their forms upwards from the abyss, and stand like lone pillars, regardless of the surge that ever lashes into foam against them. Ruins of ancient castles and forts, the residences of Chieftains of other days present themselves on the coast in the most weird situations, frequently erected over the yawning gulfs, looking down upon the tumultuous waters that roll beneath. What can be more wildly romantic than the situation of Dunleky castle, embraced within the arms of a precipice? Yet, all this wild and romantic magnificence can be viewed, not only without danger, but with the greatest possible safety and pleasure from any Irish jaunting car or other vehicle, or on foot or horseback. The road south of Kilkee to Carrigaholt, and thence to Loop-Head (22 miles) is as smooth and level as a park avenue or bowling green. To the north of Kilkee, you see the horse-shoe, cut out of the giant rock, and forming an amphitheatre, the green waters of the Atlantic being the arena. The coast runs in bold perpendicular massiveness, as an immense iron wall, the entire distance to Galway. In the vicinage of Kilkee there are numerous walks about the cliffs, and many seats, cut from the rocks, where visitors can sit for hours, viewing the boundless sea, reading, conversing or feasting.

In the month of December, 1865, a melancholy catastrophe occurred at the puffing-hole rocks. Two young lives (Col. Pepper and his affianced bride, Miss Smithwick) fell victims to the yawning vortex. They ventured out upon the overhanging rocks, during a momentary calm, when a mighty wave belched forth, and swept them off the rocks. Some years ago a ship called the Intrinsic, went down in broad noon-day, it being hemmed in, during a storm, between the rocks, within a few hundred yards from the shore.

The following neat but painful story was related by an eye witness to the event narrated:

Two gentlemen, walking beside the huge cliffs that overhang the Atlantic, some three miles south of Kilkee, were surprised to see a sheep and her little lamb cropping the verdure that grew upon a rock several hundred feet beneath the surface of the mainland. Being curious to learn how the two could return, they waited only a short time when the old sheep decided to climb back again. Having advanced about twenty yards, she encountered a large stone, whose ledge jutted forward some two or three feet. Apparently calculating from her precarious position, with surprising agility and vigor, she bounced upwards and succeeded in placing her foremost feet on the rock. With a painful struggle she endeavored to ascend, but, after a second or two, her strength failed and the creature fell backwards, and then down, and downwards from rock to rock, until at length her body struck the stony beach below, where it was rendered a quivering mass of mangled flesh. During all this time, the little lamb was a surprised spectator. With distended eyes and ears it appeared to wonder at the antics of its mother. At last, seeing its mother's form hurled over the rocky chasm, the little creature gave a wild bleat, and immediately plunged over the abyss, falling upon the mangled body of its dam. Soon a surging wave dashed over them, washing their remains into the briny deep. The gentlemen who saw the lamb plunge, declared it was a veritable case of animal suicide.

Kilkee is within easy distance of the famous Cliffs of Moher (700 feet high), and Lisdoonvarna Spa, the curative properties of whose mineral waters have acquired a world-famed repute. Besides the excellence of the springs, (sulphur, iron and magnesia) the pure mountain air of the district renders it a most desirable rendezvous for those afflicted with rheumatism, dyspepsia, liver and kidney complaints and other chronic diseases. Lisdoonvarna is especially noted for the number of its clerical visitors. Priests from all parts of the United Kingdom may be seen here during the months of July and August.*

The picnics and wagonette excursions that are gotten up at these two health resorts, afford as much innocent amusement as can be enjoyed at such feasts. On the wagonettes (each capable of holding about twenty-five persons) every occupant strives to contribute to the general mirth. If *bulls* and *puns*, merry songs and boisterous laughter indicate pleasure and delight, no other improvised entertainments can excel these entertainments.

As the quaint and witty driver whips his four-in-hand, every visible object in the landscape becomes an object of mirthful criticism. The little boys and girls that

---

* The resident Priests of these localities, Rev. E. Power, Quinlisan T. Brosnan, P. Sweeny and P. Brennan, (the latter a skillful church architect) have numerous respectable relatives in New England and other States. Their hospitality and priestly benevolence have endeared them to several American tourists.

hang on the rear steps or run after the vehicles for pennies, are often seen cuffing one another or tumbling headforemost; the climbing of the hill of the cork-screw road or fields leading to the Cliffs of Moher, and the descent, whilst a raging wind is resisting or propelling; the frequent slips and falls of good-humored ladies and gentlemen; the fantastic vagaries of the wind, blowing now a female's head-dress, muff or shawl, and again, a gent's hat or ulster, and their ludicrous efforts to recover them, all contribute to render such tours the acme of social enjoyment. But the Loop-Head light-house excites more uncontrollable laughter than any other single object. When tourists, having ascended the spiral stairs, behold the reflection of their faces on the convex and concave lenses of the great lamp that casts its illuminated rays on the waters beneath, they cannot, by any possible effort, restrain immoderate laughter. The handsomest face is so elongated or contorted as to cause its owner to despise himself for the time. Whilst the eyes and nose appear frightful, the teeth are hideous, if not appalling objects. A young lady opening her mouth to expose her pretty teeth, appeared the most ludicrous if not the most disgusting object I ever beheld.

KILKEE.

"To the West, to the West, for a dip in the sea,
Where the mighty Atlantic rolls into Kilkee;
With a breeze from the waves rolling up to your doors
As if Boreas and Neptune were stopping at Moore's.
If you go there in May, perhaps t'will be dull,
But from June to October the lodges are full;
And Erin's fair daughters find health in the wave,
Where Erin's poor emigrants once found a grave.*

* This is an allusion to the shipwreck.

To the West, to the West, for a dip in the sea,
Where the mighty Atlantic rolls into Kilkee,
The belles of Tipperary, the beauties of Clare
The Limerick lassies in summer are there.

"On the strand of Kilkee pony phaetons we meet,
And gay landaulets dashing by on the street;
We gaze with delight on the waists, taper and small,
Then whistle a 'deuxtemps' and wish for a ball;
Their picnics are plenty, though by rain sometimes marr'd,
For a drive to Loop-Head or a walk to Baltard,
To the hill called 'Look Out' or the rocks just below,
To see the waves breaking, on Sundays we go.

To the West, to the West, etc.

"In Kilkee there is love making, larking and fun;
The ladies to please, is the work to be done;
We'll try it; we'll do it, and never despair
While Moore has a room and good music is there.
Each morning fair ladies in blue baize are seen,
At evening promenade in bright bombazine,
And at night appear in their loveliest still,
As they fly through a galop or walk a quadrille;
With a breeze from the waves rolling up from the shore,
Which they could ne'er find at Kingston, Kinsale or Tramore.

To the West, to the West, etc."

LAKES OF KILLARNEY.

The Lakes are three in number, the Upper, the Lower and Middle. Although the Lower and Middle Lakes exhibit a very happy combination of the sublime and beautiful, the grand and the magnificent are more peculiarly the characteristics of their elder sister. She is embosomed in an almost voiceless solitude, her mountains are more terrific, her islands more gloomy, her dashing cataracts more astounding. The Lower Lake, however, will be apt to continue the more general favorite, from its superior expanse of waters, the multitude and beauty of its sparkling islands, rich promontories and wooded mountains, as well as from the level country that forms its boundary, on one side presenting an undulating line of mountains in soft perspective. But the principal charm of Killarney consists in its magical variety. Like the beauty of Nourmahal, it is not by a monotonous perfection that it pleases, but by an ever animated, ever changing, fascination which every mist that sleeps upon its waters, every ray that glances on its mountain tops, every breath that ruffles its bosom, every season that clothes or strips, or diversifies its mountain woods, exhibit under a new aspect of loveliness, imbued afresh with a thousand prismatic colors. Every step you take, you imagine that, like the illusive landscape that mocked whilst it enchanted the vision of the Red-Cross Knight, all the objects around you are undergoing a visible metamorphose. Not a rock, not a wave, not a tree, from the druidical oak to the diamond hung arbutus, that does not alter its aspect with the position you take, and appear as if spangled anew with a fresh coat of sparkling tints and hues; whilst the silvery mists, that rise like guardian spirits from the depths of the lakes, the fairy voices that respond at every call, the ever-moving lights and shadows, which are continually revealing or shrouding some prominent feature of the landscape, never suffer the intensity of your interest to subside. Nor is there anything incongruous in the disposition of the surrounding objects. The highlands and the valleys, the animated and the solitary regions, the still grottos and the surrounding cataracts, the wildness and the bloom, the lofty and the gentle features of the scene, blend harmoniously together. Its solemnity is always relieved by its brilliancy, and its brilliancy ever chastened by the continual presence of its awful mountains. Add to this that every rock has its legend, every island its tale of marvel.

No place else can charm the eye
  With such bright and varied tints,
Every rock that you pass by
  Verdure broiders or besprints;
Virgin there the green grass grows,
  Every morn Spring's natal day,
Bright-hued berries daff the snows,
  Smiling Winter's frown away.
Angels often pausing there,
  Doubt if Eden were more fair;
Beauty's home, Killarney,
  Ever fair Killarney.

O'Rourke.

THE ROCK OF CASHEL.

(R. C. DUNGARVAN.)

"There breathes a spirit thro' these lonely halls,
  There speaks a voice from each desert aisle,
That insensibly the musing mind recalls
  To days of yore, when from this mighty pile
Religion's flame shone bright o'er Erin's isle;
  When mitred Cormac filled the royal chair
And swayed the sceptre and the cross the while;
  Prince, sage and soldier found a dwelling there.

Who dwells there now? the hideous screaming owl,
  Her loathsome way, through each dark passage wings;
The lap-wing, swallow and raven fowl
  Are nestling in the very spot where kings

> Sat throned on high, midst court and gatherings;
> And all is still save when some wild bird's scream
> Through these lone courts with dismal echo rings
> Make sounds that haunt us in a troubled dream.
>
> Royal and saintly Cashel! I could weep
> O'er thy ruined grandeur and departed powers,
> As thy past glories, fore my mind's eye sweep
> And show how fleetly glide life's checkered hours;
> Now, from the summit of thy mouldering towers
> I gaze with sadness on the ruins beneath;
> There all proclaim how quickly time deflours
> And levels nations with the sword of death."

In the reign of King Coorc, there lived two young swine-herds who were in the habit of feeding their swine for three months of the year on the pastures round the city where there was then a forest. At Easter, these two swine-herds, while guarding the herds of the chiefs of Muskerry and Lougharden, heard the voice of an Angel, and saw a figure of indescribable beauty perched upon one of the hills, that upon which the Rock of Cashel now stands, then called Sheedrum, or the hill of the Fairy, singing canticles to God and prophesying the birth of St. Patrick. Coorc, not believing the omen, came to the rock and selected it as the noble palace of tribute, and called it Cashel. This appears to be the most plausible history of the place.

Upon this rock, for more than a hundred years, the Princes of the provinces of Ireland, with many a noble steed, and swords glittering as the stars, and many a helmet bright as the dawn, came to deposit them as a tribute of the chiefs and people of this island, to the monarchs of Cashel. But the halls of that noble pile are silent long ago; that which was once all beauty and glory, now moulders in decay. The noblest of all epic poems, the psalter of Cashel, was written here by a disciple of St. Patrick. Upon this rock, the first provincial king of Ireland was made a convert to the christian faith. Upon the occasion of his baptism, the crozier of St. Patrick falling from his hand, pierced and spiked the king's foot to the spot on which he stood, whilst he never complained, deeming it a part of the ceremony. St. Patrick miraculously healed the wound by touching it with his hand.

The rock is an elevated, detached mass of stratified lime-stone conspicuous for miles around, being 300 feet high. Cormac's chapel is one of the most interesting architectural ruins in the kingdom. It is built of hewn stone; the walls, roof and the carvings on the arches are most elegant and elaborate. The entrance to the door-way is richly moulded and ornamented with zig-zag and bead work of astonishing beauty. The erection of this chapel is ascribed to Cormac MacCullinan, at once King and Archbishop of Cashel, (who composed the celebrated Psalter 900 A. D). The Cathedral is of later date, and divine service was held in it up to the year 1752. It was a spacious cruciform structure. On the ascent to the Cathedral is a stone, on which, according to tradition, the Kings of Munster were annually inaugurated. A synod was held at Cashel by St. Patrick in the reign of Angus, who, after his conversion to the christian faith, built a church here. In 990, the place was fortified by Brian Boru. In 1372, a Parliament was held at Cashel, and in 1495, during the baronial feuds Gerald, Earl of Kildare, influenced by hostile feelings towards David Creaghe the then Archbishop, set fire to the Cathedral. In the presence of the King, he afterwards defended this outrage on the ground that he would not have set fire to it, had he not thought the Archbishop was in it at the time. In 1647, Lord Inchiquin stormed the rock and put to death all the clergy he could find. Tradition reports that the rock was deposited in its present site by Satan, who had bitten it out of the mountain range, called Sleabh-bloom in the northern part of the County Tipperary at a spot where a large gap is still to be seen and universally known as the Devil's bit. St. Patrick, the titular saint of Cashel, observing the fiend flying over him with his heavy mouthful compelled him to drop it where the Rock of Cashel now stands, and forthwith consecrated it to pious usage. Upon the rock has been erected a round tower which is still entire.

QUEENSTOWN.

The Cove, or as it is now called Queenstown, (in honor of a recent visit of Queen Victoria), was formerly called Clon-mel (sweet spot) which appears the more appropriate name, distant from Cork about twelve miles, is built on a steep hill, overlooking the Atlantic, having at present (1889) a population of 9,755 inhabitants. Its natural advantages indisputably render it the noblest asylum for shipping in Europe. A series of parallel terraces reach from the water's edge to the top of the surrounding hill, from which the naked eye can behold one of the finest marine views in the world. Its happy situation near the sea, and the salubrity and equability of its climate render it one of the most desirable health resorts in the kingdom.

Nothing can be more enchanting than to proceed by

land or water from Cork to Queenstown. It has been an undecided question whether Killarney, with its lakes, mountains, woods, and water-falls, is calculated to fill the mind with nobler thoughts and lovelier images of land and water scenery. When the tide is in, the Lee appears a most beautiful river, rivalling the Blackwater in the romantic points of its course from its source in the sublime and sacred lake of Gougaune Barra, until it mingles its waters with the sea at Queenstown. Let us take the journey by water from Cork to Queenstown. On the left, as you proceed down the river, are the wooded heights of Glanmire, crimsoned with numerous fairy-like villas and mansions; on the right, a landscape equally beautiful, as we pass by Black Rock castle and Monkstown. The great fascination of the trip by water to Queenstown, arises from the sinuous windings of the river Lee by which frequent changes of scenery are presented to view; shady groves, ancient castles, picturesque villages and the tall masts of ships present themselves before us. We approach the beautiful town of Passage where merchant vessels ride at anchor; but when we turn Battery Point and behold the noble harbor of Queenstown spreading before us with its fortified islets, undulated hills and terraced walks, we feel it is magnificent and charming scenery. The largest fleet of the British navy could find shelter within its bay. Towering over all the buildings of the city stands the great Cathedral of St. Colman. When complete, the cross on the spire of this noble edifice will be the last object seen by the departing emigrant; whilst its golden armlets will be the first beacon to gladden the anxious eye of the returning exile.

Perhaps there is not another spot on the surface of

the globe that reveals a sadder picture than the harbor of Queenstown. Here, the links that bind parents, brethren, dearest friends and affianced lovers are drawn to their utmost tension.

When we consider that even the savage loves his native home, what must be the emotions of a tender-hearted and spirited peasantry when here they must part, perhaps forever, from those they love? On the tranquil bosom of this lovely shore, millions of Irishmen in America, living and dead, have slept for the last time, and have shed their last tears on Irish soil.

The heart-rending wails, prayers and tearful farewells that have been uttered here, have no counterpart in the history of the human family. Fifty thousand is the average number of emigrants that embark from this harbor every year!

> "O bewitching scene! O blissful home,
> Amongst your paths I'd love to roam;
> And ponder o'er those faded days
> Whose memory casts her brightest rays;
> And nought but the Atlantic's roar
> I'd hear by your pebbly shore,
> Save the wild pigeon's cooing note
> Or bleating of the mountain goat."

IRISH MINSTRELSY.

THE IRISH BALLAD SINGER.*

CONSIDERING the dearth of current literature in Ireland, no public character-writer, poet or orator, has contributed more towards the maintenance and development of ethnical characteristics than the Irish ballad singer.

Parading along the thoroughfares of the large cities and streets of the country villages, he never failed to extol chivalry and virtue and denounce national apostasy and crime; his bosom heaved as he chanted the noble deeds of patriots and philanthropists, whilst a wrathful scowl overshadowed his manly brow as he recounted the shameful misdeeds of tyranny and oppression. The sorrows, sufferings and aspirations of the nation were chanticleered with a pathos that often excited the most ardent enthusiasm in the breasts of his auditors. In some respects, the burden of the ballad singer's notes appeared to be anomalous; the Judge and Jury were frequently assailed in words of scathing reproof, whilst the victim condemned to the gallows was panegyrized as though he were a martyr and not a capital criminal. This will appear intelligible when we

---

* "Give me the ballads of a nation, and I care not who made its laws."—*A. Fletcher.*

consider how often so-called "Law and Order" have been perverted by the ruling classes in Ireland.

That of the ballad singer, standing in the midst of some public square or street corner, surrounded by an ever increasing motley crowd, holding a string of ballads, and between notes doffing his hat at a recognized acquaintance, or winking at the pretty girls wedged amongst the crowd, is a picture novel as it is interesting. Frequently, before his song was ended, the crowd vociferously applauding, his enthusiasm overleaped the limits of measured harmony. Indeed, such poets as Moore, Goldsmith and Thomas Duffet minimized the wild refrain of Irish minstrelsy. A rattling, reckless extravagance, a dare-devil humor most frequently characterized the improvised notes of the Irish ballad singer, and gave them the racial pathos that rendered them so striking and picturesque. "The Fair Hills of Ireland," "The Wearing of the Green," "The Cruiskeen Lawn," and the "Sprig of Shillelagh," furnished full scope to his fertile imagination. At fairs, patterns and races the ballad singer's voice was loudest and clearest.

Although the following cannot be considered a typical specimen of Irish Minstrelsy, still, the fact that it excited the wrath of the Tory government to impose a sentence of three months' imprisonment (Dec. '89) on a poor ballad singer and his wife who dared to sing it in public, we trust, will be ample apology for its insertion:

I.

Mother, alanna, don't be crying though I am far away
From the cottage where you reared me and where I used to play,
Better times are shortly coming to alleviate our woe,
And we'll all embark for Ireland when the landlords go.

II.

The landlord compensated you with very slender purse,
He heeded not the widow's wail nor the orphan's curse,
He thought to get the farm till the Land League told him no-
But we'll all go home to Ireland when the landlords go.

III.

Though I'm far away from Ireland, still the farm try and keep;
It was salted well with rent, but now it's very cheap;
The only tenants are the rats, the jackdaw, and the crow,
So we'll all go home to Ireland when the landlords go.

IV.

The Land League is shielding you from every hurt and harm—
There's not a man in Ireland would take a widow's farm—
There's no one found to till the ground, nor yet the crop to sow—
So we'll all go back to Ireland when the landlords go.

An anecdote, published by a veteran of the late American war will suffice to show the popularity of the following ballad composed by the patriot T. D. Sullivan. It was the evening before the great battle of Fredericksburg. The federal army lay under arms all night saddened by the loss of so many brave comrades. Captain Downing, an Irishman, commenced to chant this favorite song; the refrain of the first couplet was taken up and chorused by his regiment, then by the brigade, again by the division and finally by the entire army line, extending a distance of six miles. When the captain had ended the song he was more than surprised to hearken to his song echoed back by the confederate lines on the opposite side of the river.

SONG FROM THE BACKWOODS.

T. D. SULLIVAN, 1857.

Deep in Canadian woods we've met,
  From one bright island flown;
Great is the land we tread, but yet
  Our hearts are with our own.
And ere we leave this shanty small,
    While fades the autumn day,
      We'll toast old Ireland! dear old Ireland!
    Ireland, boys, hurra!

We've heard her faults a hundred times,
  The new ones and the old,
In songs and sermons, rants and rhymes,
  Enlarged some fifty-fold.
But take them all, the great and small,
    And this we've got to say:—
      Here's dear old Ireland! good old Ireland!
    Ireland, boys, hurra.

We know that brave and good men tried
  To snap her rusty chain,
That patriots suffered, martyrs died,
  And all, 'tis said, in vain;
But no, boys, no! a glance will show
    How far they've won their way—
      Here's good old Ireland! loved old Ireland!
    Ireland, boys, hurra!

We've seen the wedding and the wake,
  The patron and the fair;
The stuff they take, the fun they make,
  And the heads they break down there,
With a loud "hurroo" and a "pillalu,"
    And a thundering "clear the way!"
      Here's gay old Ireland! dear old Ireland!
    Ireland, boys, hurra!

And well we know in the cool grey eves,
  When the hard day's work is o'er,
How soft and sweet are the words that greet
  The friends who meet once more;
With "Mary machree!" and "My Pat! 'tis he!"
  And "My own heart night and day!"
    Ah, fond old Ireland! dear old Ireland!
    Ireland, boys, hurra!

And happy and bright are the groups that pass
  From their peaceful homes, for miles
O'er fields, and roads, and hills, to Mass,
  When Sunday morning smiles!
And deep the zeal their true hearts feel
  When low they kneel and pray.
    O, dear old Ireland! blest old Ireland!
    Ireland, boys, hurra!

But deep in Canadian woods we've met,
  And we never may see again
The dear old isle where our hearts are set,
  And our first fond hopes remain!
But come, fill up another cup,
  And with every sup let's say—
    Here's loved old Ireland! good old Ireland!
    Ireland, boys, hurra!

That national apostasy militates against the genius and spirit of the nation may be seen from the following insertion. In the memorable year of '98, a young man, the leader of a secret band of insurgents was captured. He was offered pardon if he would turn king's evidence by giving the names of his accomplices. His mother, hearing that he was wavering, and fearing lest he should turn informer, addressed him in the following strain:

THE PATRIOT MOTHER.

A BALLAD OF '98.

"Come, tell us the name of the rebelly crew,
 Who lifted the pike on the Curragh with you;
 Come, tell us the treason, and then you'll be free,
 Or right quickly you'll swing from the high gallows tree."

"*Alanna! alanna!* the shadow of shame
 Has never yet fallen upon one of your name,
 And O! may the food from my bosom you drew,
 In your veins turn to poison, if *you* turn untrue.

"The foul words—O! let them not blacken your tongue,
 That would prove to your friends and your country a wrong,
 Or the curse of a mother, so bitter and dread,
 With the wrath of the Lord—may they fall on your head!

"I have no one but you in the whole world wide,
 Yet false to your pledge, you'd ne'er stand at my side:
 If a traitor you lived, you'd be farther away
 From my heart than, if true, you were wrapped in the clay.

"O! deeper and darker the mourning would be,
 For your falsehood so base, than your death proud and free,
 Dearer, far dearer than ever to me,
 My darling, you'll be on the brave gallows tree!

" Tis holy, agra, from the bravest and best—
 Go! go! from my heart, and be joined with the rest,
 Alanna machree! O alanna machree!*
 Sure a 'stag'† and a traitor you never will be."

There's no look of a traitor upon the young brow
 That's raised to the tempters so haughtily now;
 No traitor e'er held up the firm head so high—
 No traitor e'er show'd such a proud flashing eye.

* *A leanbh mo chroidhe*—O child of my heart.
† "Stag," an informer.

On the high gallows tree! on the brave gallows tree!
Where smiled leaves and blossoms, his sad doom met he!
But it never bore blossom so pure or so fair
As the heart of the martyr that hangs from it there.

The following ballad recalls the lines of Virgil,* "*auri per ramos aura refulget*," where the pure gold of womanly devotion and purity shines through the modest foliage which surround it:

NICE LITTLE JENNIE FROM BALLINASLOE.

(STREET BALLAD).

You lads that are funny, and call maids your honey,
Give ear for a moment, I'll not keep you long;
I'm wounded by Cupid, he has made me quite stupid,
To tell you the truth now, my brain's nearly wrong;
A neat little posy, who lives quite cosy,
Has kept me unable to walk to and fro;
Each day I'm declining, in love I'm repining,
For nice little Jenny from Ballinasloe.

It was in September, I'll ever remember,
I went out to walk by a clear river side
For sweet recreation, but, to my vexation,
This wonder of Nature I quickly espied;
I stood for to view her an hour I'm sure;
The earth could not show such a damsel, I know,
As that little girl, the pride of the world,
Called nice little Jenny from Ballinasloe.

I said to her: "Darling! this is a nice morning;
The birds sing enchanting, which charms the groves;
Their notes do delight me, and you do invite me,
Along this clear water some time for to rove;

---

* Æneid lib. 6, v. 204.

Your beauty has won me, and surely undone me,
If you won't agree for to cure my sad woe,
So great is my sorrow, I'll ne'er see to-morrow,
My sweet little Jenny from Ballinasloe."

"Sir, I did not invite you, nor yet dare slight you;
You're at your own option to act as you please;
I am not ambitious, nor e'er was officious,
I am never inclined to disdain or to tease;
I love conversation, likewise recreation,
I'm free with a friend, and I'm cold with a foe;
But virtue's my glory, and will be till I'm hoary,"—
Said nice little Jenny from Ballinasloe.

"Most lovely of creatures! your beautiful features
Have sorely attracted and captured my heart;
If you won't relieve me, in truth you may believe me,
Bewildered in sorrow till death I must smart;
I'm at your election, so grant me protection,
And feel for a creature that's tortured in woe;
One smile it will heal me; one frown it will kill me;
Sweet, nice little Jenny from Ballinasloe!"

"Sir, yonder's my lover, if he should discover
Or ever take notice you spoke unto me,
He'd close your existence in spite of resistance;
Be pleased to withdraw, then, lest he might you see;
You see he's approaching, then don't be encroaching,
He has his large dog and his gun there also;
Although you're a stranger I wish you from danger,"
Said nice little Jenny from Ballinasloe.

I bowed then genteelly, and thanked her quite freely;
I bid her adieu and took to the road;
So great was my trouble my pace I did double;
My heart was oppressed and sank down with the load;
For ever I'll mourn for beauteous Jane Curran,
And ramble about in affection and woe,
And think on the hour I saw that sweet flower,—
My dear little Jenny from Ballinasloe!

"The whole history of Irish subjugation and its seven centuries of successive struggles," says a distinguished historian,* begins with the carrying off of Devorgilla, wife of Tiernan O'Rourke, King of Breffni by a dissolute giant, Desmond Macmurrough, King of Leinster. Through ages of bondage and slaughter the country has indeed bled for her shame." One might paraphrase the words of Shakespeare's Diomed in Troilus and Cressida; "that for every false drop in her bawdy veins, an English life hath sunk; and for every scruple of her contaminated carrion weight an Irishman was slain." The Lord of Breffni made war on his betrayer. Dermot fled to England where his cause was espoused by King Henry II. At the time, the only Englishman who ever occupied the papal chair, Adrian IV, was Pope.

It is said that the English King obtained from this Pope a bull, authorizing him to invade Ireland, which he represented as an "uncivilized and barbarous nation." Whilst historians do not agree in their opinions concerning the issue of such a papal mandate, it is certain that Henry, availing himself of Desmond's quarrel, sent over to Ireland an army of Norman barons headed by Richard de Clare, commonly called Strongbow,† who succeeded in subduing the Irish clans and placing the country under English rule, for the first time.

Before the invasion, Ireland was divided into four confederate tribes: the O'Neils of Ulster, the O'Connors of Connaught, the MacMurroughs of Leinster and the O'Briens and MacCarthys of Munster. After the invasion, the Normans soon swarmed over the country, forcing their strange names and strange ways into the

---

* Justin MacCarthy. † A. D. 1170.

homes of the time-honored Septs. De Burgos, Fitzmaurices, Fitzgeralds, De Laceys, De Courcys and Mandevilles were to be the new masters of those who were heretofore ruled by the lords of the O and the Mac.

There is a grim ironic mockery in the thought that two nations have been for centuries set in the bitterest hatred by the behavior of a lusty savage and an unfaithful wife.

The following beautiful poem from the pen of Moore, refers to this painful event:

THE SONG OF O'RUARK,

PRINCE OF BREFFNI.

The valley lay smiling before me,
  Where lately I left her behind;
Yet I trembled, and something hung o'er me
  That sadden'd the joy of my mind.
I look'd for the lamp which, she told me,
  Should shine when her pilgrim* return'd;
But, though darkness began to enfold me,
  No lamp from the battlements burn'd.

I flew to her chamber—'twas lonely,
  As if the loved tenant lay dead;—
Ah, would it were death, and death only!
  But no, the young false one had fled.
And there hung the lute that could soften
  My very worst pains into bliss,
While the hand that had waked it so often
  Now throbb'd to a proud rival's kiss.

---

* O'Rourke went on a pilgrimage, an act of piety frequent in those days.

There *was* a time, falsest of women!
　When Breffni's good sword would have sought
That man, through a million of foemen,
　Who dared but to wrong thee *in thought!*
While now—O degenerate daughter
　Of Erin, how fallen is thy fame!
And through ages of bondage and slaughter,
　Our country shall bleed for thy shame.

Already the curse is upon her,
　And strangers her valleys profane;
They come to divide—to dishonor,
　And tyrants they long will remain.
But onward!—the green banner rearing,
　Go, flesh every sword to the hilt;
On *our* side is Virtue and Erin,
　On *theirs* is the Saxon and Guilt.

The following account of the passage of the "Union" does more credit to the diplomacy than integrity of the British Parliament:

THE UNION.

SLIABH CUILINN.

How did they pass the Union?
　By perjury and fraud;
By slaves who sold their land for gold,
　As Judas sold his God;
By all the savage acts that yet
　Have followed England's track—
The pitchcap and the bayonet,
　The gibbet and the rack.
　　And thus was passed the Union,
　　　By Pitt and Castlereagh;
　　Could Satan send for such an end
　　　More worthy tools than they?

How thrive we by the Union?
  Look round our native land;
In ruined trade and wealth decayed
  See slavery's surest brand;
Our glory as a nation gone;
  Our substance drained away;
A wretched province trampled on,
  Is all we've left to-day.
    Then curse with me the Union,
      That juggle foul and base—
    The baneful root that bore such fruit
      Of ruin and disgrace.

And shall it last, this Union,
  To grind and waste us so?
O'er hill and lea, from sea to sea,
  All Ireland thunders, No!
Eight million necks are stiff to bow—
  We know our might as men;
We conquered once before, and now
  We'll conquer once again,
    And rend the cursed Union,
      And fling it to the wind—
    And Ireland's laws in Ireland's cause
      Alone our hearts shall bind!

NATIONAL TRAITS AND CHARACTER.

BEFORE closing the pages of this little volume, we would indite a few remarks concerning the present inhabitants of Ireland. Although our assumptions may appear gratuitous and rather bold, nevertheless, we venture to insert them.

No matter how copious the quotations from other authors may be, we think a descriptive writer should record his own observations, even though they may not always be unimpeachable. Accordingly, we assure the reader that no motive shall induce us to suppress facts, however humiliating, or assert traits that are more flattering than pertinent to the national character. Having sojourned in Ireland (my native country) during the greater parts of the years '88 and '89, after a residence of almost a quarter of a century in the United States, I presume my allegations are as trustworthy as might be expected from an impartial and careful observer.

Like other nations, the Irish have their virtues* and their vices. Their virtues we cannot recommend in more forcible language than to affirm that an upright Irishman is one of the noble specimens of the human family; your life, your virtue and your wealth you may unhesitatingly entrust to his care. On the other hand,

---

* "Her virtues are her own, her vices were forced upon her."—*R. Holmes.*

there are some vices and failings still prevalent, that no true Irishman or christian can endorse.

Ireland has furnished arch-traitors* (perhaps, has some within her bosom to-day) equally reprobate with Benedict Arnold and Titus Oates. The most notorious informers and vile apostates Ireland ever knew, were some of her own ungrateful children. The infamous James Cary, Richard Pigott and Delaney were Irishmen. The scurrilous pamphlet, "*Parnellism and Crime*," we regret to say, was penned by an Irish hand. At present, an Irish ex-M. P. is conniving at, if not abetting the efforts that are being made to incriminate the leader and chief representative of the Irish nation.

'But we would not dare asperse the national character by such insignificant exceptions. Ireland, compared with other nations, can produce a glorious record. The religious or national apostasy of a few of her sons and daughters does not tarnish the nation's integrity, no more than a decayed branch or a withered leaf disfigures the symmetry of the sturdy oak.

Ireland, to-day, is a veritable repository of uncompromising virtue. A stranger landing on its green shores, can sniff with the aroma of fragrant hawthorns and furze blossoms, the sweet odor of purity and unvarnished charity; he finds what is difficult to be found elsewhere—virtue mantled in *purple* as well as clothed in rags.

Naturally averse to hypocrisy and political chicanery, the fair gifts wherewith nature has blessed the Irish

---

* "Let Erin remember the days of old
    Ere faithless sons betrayed her."—*Moore*.

people permit them to dispense with religious and social tinsel. Neither the wardrobe nor the money chest forestalls the merits of an Irish woman or man in his native land.

The foregoing remarks might be said to represent the general outlines of Irish character at the present day. We shall now beg to particularize our comments by reviewing Irish traits in their social, physical and religious aspect. To render our description plainer, we shall institute a comparison between the inhabitants of Ireland and America.

SOCIAL CHARACTERISTICS.

Socially, it is not surprising that America, to which all European nations contribute the best brain, bone and sinew, should far out-rival the motherland. Whilst the poor emigrant from Erin is dubbed "the *green horn*" for a year or two after landing, an American is everywhere reputed a citizen of the world. Priests in Ireland have frequently observed that men or women who have lived some years in America exhibit more business tact and enterprise than other members, not only of the family, but of the entire parish. Whether it is complimentary or otherwise, the peasantry appear very exact when dealing with a "*Yankee.*"

A country of great mountains, rivers, lakes and commerce, is naturally expected to be a country of great people. The intellectual refinement and suave deportment; the air of non-obtrusive confidence and resolve, perceptible in the looks of the American youth entitle them to converse with the highest grades of society from which the lack of social intercourse debars a plurality of Irish native residents.

Whilst the masses of the American people are generally less educated, they are unquestionably more gallant and sentimental than their Irish or British cousins. Although "Brother Jonathan" has been frequently taunted for his inordinate love of the "*Almighty Dollar,*"* a careful observer would notice that "John Bull" seldom fails to prefer the wealth of pounds, shillings and pence to any other wealth of nature or virtue that a man or woman can possess. The "Maid of Erin," too, casts a loving glance at the "Queen's Head" in current specie. An Irish shopkeeper or farmer never dreams of marrying a girl solely for the graces of her saintly life and the figure of her handsome face; he generally selects one who can produce "*figures*" from her purse. Romance, then, is not an Irish or an English commodity. In all parts of Great Britain and Ireland society is segregated into three grand divisions, designated first, second and third class. Class No. 1 never associates with class No. 2, whilst a member of class No. 3 would be considered audacious if he were to aspire to any number but 3. Those *shoddy aristocrats* who ignore this fixity of caste, and who attempt to *put on* society manners after they have fastened their boots and gloves, are invariably pointed out by the finger of scorn or ridicule.

In pursuing our "*social*" criticism, we would mention a few other faults and unsavory customs of the Irish at home. Whilst the lack of industry is not to be wondered at, owing to the stagnant pulse of domestic enterprise, the fact that the independent habits of the people indicate unwarranted pride is unaccountable, as it is

---

* The term originated with Washington Irving as a satire on the American love of gain.

unpraiseworthy. The poorest farmer or merchant, no matter how numerous his family or imminent his wants, will not permit any member to labor for hire or work outside his own premises. We allow there are some exceptions, but it is painful that we must classify them as such.

Whilst I would not dare asperse my countrymen with the taunt of intemperance, I must positively aver there are a vast percentage too many liquor shops in every city and country village of Ireland. Of course there is the old palliative excuse that the people must be lucratively employed in some business. I do not insinuate that intoxication is more prevalent in Ireland than America, I simply assert that there is urgent cause to propagate the League of the Cross in Ireland.

The worst feature about intemperance in Ireland is that it does not disgust popular sentiment as in America. Even some of the fair sex display remarkable potulent capabilities. It is nothing extraordinary to see jaunty and genteel young ladies enter a coffee or drawing-room and call for wines and ciders or other stronger spirituous stimulants, and nonchalantly deposit them within their dainty bosoms. In America, a lady would be considered *bold* to make such an attempt, even with the aid of a straw and considerable handkerchief sneezing. In America, a drunken man is universally regarded a dangerous brute; in Ireland, he is usually wheedled, and considers himself more advanced than his "fellows."

Before this vice can be rooted out of the country, we are sorry to say public sentiment, male and female, must be reversed. The recent attitude of the patriotic Archbishop of Dublin (Most Rev. Dr. Walsh) refusing to attend a meeting designing to erect a statue of Father

Mathew in Dublin, appears to endorse our allegation. The following insertion is an extract from the venerable Archbishop's letter to Mayor Sexton, Oct. 10, 1889:

"The erection of a statue of Father Mathew is not the proper way just now to honor his memory. Let us rather make some vigorous efforts to perpetuate his work. Until that is done, and done with a substantial measure of success, a statue of Father Mathew would only serve as a standing record of reproach to all. The lesson taught by certain *statistics* recently published is, that one of the most *urgent needs* of our day in Ireland is the establishment of national organizations for the suppression of intemperance."

When we consider that the government withholds almost all lucrative employments from Irish Catholics, it is a matter of surprise to find the vast majority of the people so temperate. It is a fearful arraignment to allege that the attitude of the present government positively encourages the liquor traffic and intemperance in Ireland. This is villainous policy and should herald the death-knell of the party capable of such infamy.

The next abuse which custom has sanctioned in Ireland, the employment of young women in the sale of intoxicants, is so prevalent that we shall devote a special tract to its discussion.

AN IRISH BAR-MAID.

In many first, and almost all second-class hotels in Ireland, after a tourist or traveller has engaged sitting and sleeping compartments, it is customary that all subsequent arrangements shall be negotiated with the Bar-Maid. She is an agreeable and ever accessible conductor of business and gossip.

As Bar-Maids who are in requisition must be well educated, and possessed of refined and engaging manners, it follows that no ill-tempered or coarse-mannered woman can maintain the office. The more charming her physique, and insinuating her wit, the more suitable she is for the position.*

The duties of an efficient Bar-Maid are manifold and sometimes infeasible. Besides being an expert in the distribution of cordials, cigars and matches, she is betimes expected to pose as an avowed Nationalist, an out-spoken Liberal, and *occasionally*, a reserved Tory; hence, she is expected to possess an inexhaustible store of patience, coquetry and slang. She must duly record day and date of boarders' arrival, and in well-rounded chirography, indite every chargeable service in their "bill." Although never called by her christian name, such as Mary, Kate or Rose, she is always expected to promptly respond when addressed patronymically Miss A, B, or C. She is cognizant of the idiosyncrasies as well as the normal humor of each inmate; whilst with the employed members of the household, she is an acknowledged favorite. An eligible Bar-Maid must be always marriageable and under thirty; must have a pair of bright, laughing eyes, incapable of wincing or frowning at any double-meaning remark or improvident exposure; ears, ready to hearken to good or evil report, equally indifferent to prayers and curses, hymns or profane ditties; nasal organs, not over-sensitive in the

---

* The following notice appeared in the "want" column of the Dublin "Freeman" of 1889:—

BAR-MAID WANTED.—Good appearance indispensible. Send Photo and address.

presence of uncorked, souring bottles and belching stomachs. Although her position entitles her to repel labial or manual familiarity with her rosy cheeks, her soft white hand must not be too quickly withdrawn from the rude or lecherous grasp of a customer. Her tongue, like her ungloved hand, must neither be too frisky nor too reserved; it is expected to join occasionally in the unlicensed chorus of ribaldry and persiflage. The Bar-Maid would be unfit for her position should she attempt to retort any insinuation, however obscene or sarcastic, addressed to her by gentlemen patrons.

The Bar-Maid, like the wandering courtesan, can succeed only while she is young and handsome. When wrinkles furrow into her velvet dimples, and silver threads commingle with her raven or flaxen hair, she is no longer suitable for the bar. If her accumulated savings are not competent to support her in the winter of her age, she need not appeal to the philanthropy of those who once patronized her *counter*. The aged Bar-Maid, like a faded rose in a crystal epergne, is invariably cast away and the vacancy re-filled by a fresh and blooming substitute.*

It redounds to the chivalry of our people that no respectable young woman is permitted to fill such a degrading position in America. It is an unmitigated shame, that in two such christian countries as Ireland and England (Scotland has no Bar-Maids) that a refined and innocent girl should be constrained to fill such an unsavory and loathsome occupation. In the name of Irish maiden-hood and national modesty, we would en-

---

* A respectable Bar-Maid assured the Author that her *dismissal* was caused by the *application* of a younger and a handsomer girl.

treat that young women be no longer employed as Bar-Maids in Ireland.†

A stranger conversant with the Irish peasantry cannot fail to notice considerable difference, if not covert hostility entertained by not a few of the inhabitants towards the national cause. Several Priests and prominent land-leaguers have declared that the national movement has been frequently marred by personal or local quarrels and petty jealousies, and that it required all their energy to keep the masses of the people banded together. Although the abstract of landlordism has been the greatest curse that ever afflicted the Irish race, yet there are in Ireland at the present day, farmers and shop-keepers who, like Esau, would sell their national birth-right for a "*mess of pottage;*" men who, for a paltry reduction of rent, or the offer of a cheap house or farm, would trample upon their country's noblest aspirations.

During my recent visit to Ireland I have frequently heard men and women attribute selfish motives to the *sayings* and *doings* of members of Parliament, newspaper editors and prominent Home Rulers. Even those who were cast into prison did not escape their vindictive

---

† Lest the foregoing criticism should be misconstrued, we beg to state that by its insertion, we had no intention to cast obloquy on the many respectable young ladies who fill this position in Ireland. Like a majority of their countrywomen, their behavior is above hostile criticism. We simply attack the *office*—not those who fill the office of Bar-Maid. Last summer, two respectable gentlemen still living in Ireland, happened to be engaged in a room adjacent to a Bar, and accidentally overhearing part of the language spoken in the presence of the young lady at the Bar, declared they would rather see their sisters dead than become Bar-Maids. These gentlemen sympathized with the young lady and enthusiastically admired her forbearance and modesty.

vituperation. The same suspicious spirit prevails to some extent in this country also. An Irishman who was elected Mayor of a large city in the United States once assured me that before and during his term in office, his greatest enemies were his own countrymen. Men who were most obsequious to his predecessor (a bigoted Orangeman) often left him meditating on their parting words—"that he was nothing better than a *Donegal pedlar.*" Even if those men who have gained national notoriety in Ireland had selfish motives (which we disbelieve) they have not thereby forfeited their claim to national commendation.

In all the business affairs of life, men are supposed to have selfish motives. The engineer who drives the train; the captain who directs the steamboat; the doctor or preacher who parts his hair in the middle; men in every avenue of enterprise have motives which might be considered selfish. It makes no difference. As long as they keep on the straight course; whilst they perform faithfully the duties of their profession, it is unfair to impugn their motives. The man who lends his strength to keep the "*wheel*" moving, no matter what his thoughts, words or desires may be, deserves approbation, and even applause if his efforts are extraordinary.

Although we have mentioned these failings, we honestly aver they are not national characteristics. It is only base-minded, insignificant apostates who entertain such sinister views of their countrymen; they are as a few broken links in the national chain; putrid sores, visible not on the face, hands or feet, but festering on the posterior regions of the nation.

A few other abuses, chiefly occurring at *wakes* and *weddings*, and which afforded a theme for the vile satires of such romancers as Carleton and Lever, must not be overlooked. It is unpardonable extravagance, besides a shame to supply the numerous persons who attend wakes with liquors, snuff, pipes and tobacco. We are pleased to state that the old custom of story-telling and chanting the *Caione* by disinterested mourners is becoming obsolete, except in certain rural districts. Inviting twenty, and sometimes thirty couples to poor weddings incurs further reprehensible extravagance.

There are some other national characteristics, which although occasionally productive of good, nevertheless, do not appear to harmonize with the dictates of justice and christian charity. A pertinent instance is where the public sins of a parent or other member of a family are visited upon the children—often to the second and third generations. The accidental good that may result from the popular odium of murder, robbery, adultery or other great crimes, is not sufficient warranty to cause innocent persons to suffer.

Another unseemly custom is that of parents giving all their real and personal property to their children on the occasion of their marriage. The prevalence of this custom may be attributed to the cruel regulations of landlords who forbade a dual ownership or partition of their lands. It is a hardship—perhaps a sin against justice that, in the winter of their lives, parents should be required to yield the fruit of their life-long industry, and become dependent on the whimsical smiles and frowns of affianced relatives.

Tipping hotel-waiters, chamber-maids and "*boots*" is also a distasteful British custom to which no lady or gentleman should be subjected. It is a scurvy advantage masters take of their servants when they diminish their wages, leaving them to recoup the deficit from tourists and travelers. If the servants' fees were equable, the practice would not be so objectionable; but they usually fluctuate, being higher or lower in different hotels and on certain occasions. Hence, American tourists have often been exposed to insolence for having failed to furnish these expectative dues.

Amongst Irish social nuisances, the jarvey or jaunting car driver is entitled to particular notice. Whilst a drive on an ordinary jaunting-car affords about as little comfort as a ride on a rusty bicycle, the driver is never satisfied until he obtains a full history of the passenger's past life and future intentions. The duration and geniality of the conversation usually represent the amount of his fare. Whilst pretending to be an infallible exponent of politics and romance, we compliment his veracity by acknowledging his power of imagery to be amazingly fertile and flexible.

In no country of the world, perhaps, are the idiosyncrasies of certain individuals more noticeable than in Ireland. Here, you meet the humorous wag, with head gear either on his poll or completely covering his forehead and eyes; the English or would be English snob, with a single eye-glass, twirling a gold or silver mounted cane and preceded by a pampered spaniel which appears to be his guide. But for effeminate and arrogant pomposity, an eccentric Irish sergeant major caps the climax. The habiliments of an ordinary circus clown are commonplace compared with his bespangled uniform, divided by a silken sash and subdivided into manifold sections, outlined with orange braid and brass buttons; his rubicund breast bears gold and silver medals; a glittering sword dangles by his side; his gold banded cap (about the size of a tiny tea cup) is securely strapped to his ear, whilst his nether garments are ready to burst with a superabundance of "*Her Majesty's*" flesh. Seeing squadrons of those fellows passing through the country villages in pairs, I often wondered how the donkeys (which are captious rascals) could restrain their vociferous propensities.

We now approach the most knotty question:

PHYSIQUE AND PHYSICAL CHARACTERISTICS.

Having premised that the best brain, bone and sinew of all nations emigrate to America, and recollecting that some sixty thousand natives leave Ireland for America every year, the compliment is mutually flattering to both countries. It must, however, be allowed that native-born Irishmen at home or abroad are capable of more physical endurance than those born in this Continent.

As in all parts of Ireland the whims of caste have separated the people into various classes, differing each from each, so their forms and features are shapen or distorted. Indeed, in no other country of the world might one distinguish such a variety in a single race. Here, you see the fairest specimens and the most repulsive caricatures of humanity; the bright and laughing faces of purse-proud aristocracy riding through bare-footed and bare-handed deformity.

While nature and society appear to smile on one, they seem to frown on another class; shrivelled men and women, wanting color and calor, and whose hairs have been blanched by the bitter winters of bye-gone generations of poverty and oppression, vested in rags and eating and drinking what would offend their high-born neighbors' dogs. Poetic imagery fails to picture certain enchanting villas, stately mansions and happy homes, whilst again you would find the most squalid hovels, inhabited by colonies of haggard and hungry looking faces.

We presume the reader will be pleased to endorse the following description of the "fair sex" by William M. Thackeray, an English Protestant, whose writings reveal but little sympathy for the Irish. (Sketch Book, p. 58):

"I never saw, in any country, more general grace of manner and ladyhood. In the midst of their gaiety, they are the chastest of women. They excel the French and English ladies, not only in wit and vivacity, but also in song and music. There is something peculiarly tender and pleasing in the looks of the peasantry. I am bound to say that on rich or poor shoulders I never saw so many beautiful faces in my life. And lest the fair public may have a bad opinion of their laughing and romping, and awful levity, let it be said that with all this laughing and romping, there are no more innocent girls in the world than the Irish girls. The women of our squeamish country are far more liable to err."

We will conclude our *"physical"* discussion by a brief reference to

THE IRISH BROGUE.

Those specimens of brogue that are represented on the stage, revealing faulty orthography and worse syntax, are painful caricatures of our mother tongue. Except Joseph Murphy, Dion Boucicault and J. K. Emmet, almost all other modern dramatists furnish spurious, if not vile renditions of Irish brogue. "*'Pon me sowl oi nivver tould yez nothin ov the loike.*" To palm such a sentence for Irish brogue betrays lamentable ignorance or malice; it is counterfeiting gold with brass.

The Irish who communicate their thoughts in such jargon are but a sparse minority of the populace—poor peasants to whom Providence has denied the advantages afforded you and I, fair reader. But as wine is kept in earthen better than shining brass vessels, so many of those poor creatures have preserved faith and purity, when those who could wield the pen and harmoniously vibrate the piano keys, have lost many of the precious jewels entrusted to them by their Maker.

Hoping the reader will pardon this digression, we will resume the thread of our subject. In every country as well as Ireland, there are those who have but an imperfect knowledge of the standard tongue. In England, there is the haughty Cockney who pronounces '*orse* for horse, *hoats* for oats, *baibee* for baby; the horny-handed Highlander substitutes *kirk* for church, *bairn* for child and *mon* for man. A Welchman would not be understood in London or Edinburgh. But then it may be objected that our comments only refer to provincialisms, dialects or patois. Exactly so! The corrupt English that is spoken in certain parts of Ireland might be classified in like manner. But the brogue is entirely a different feature; it bears no relation to the grammatical constituents, but rather to the intonation of language. The Irish brogue when properly emphasized, is the most fascinating embellishment of the Celtic, English, Latin or any other tongue which it modulates; it is to language what leaves are to a tree, or flowers to a rose bush. It is a false notion to suppose it inseparable from "*Blarney*;" on the contrary, it can never assimilate with hypocrisy, since it is telephoned only through the tenderest chords of the Irish heart.

The English language is never spoken with more

pathos and eloquence than when flavored with the racy pith of the Irish brogue.

Having located *social* and *physical* facts, we now purpose to indite some brief remarks concerning

THE ASPECT OF RELIGION IN IRELAND.

In order to render our comments more intelligible we shall again beg to extend our comparison between the merits of the inhabitants of the New and the Old country. Although conceding to the Irish at home the encomiums due to their unswerving maintenance and profession of Catholicism, nevertheless, we consider there are several instances of practical faith wherein Catholics of the United States surpass them. American Catholics are *manual* rather than *labial* worshipers--in plainer words, while they pray less, they disburse more towards the support of religion and the suffrage of the "departed."

While admitting there are numerous cases of oppression and poverty in Ireland that have no counterpart in this country, it cannot be said that Catholics there are less able to contribute. Taking a bird's-eye-view of both countries, we find that churches, convents and schools in Ireland are far superior to those of this country, whilst they are invariably free from mortgages and debts. The system of dowry which Irish parents are expected to furnish at the marriage of their children, may be regarded as the chief ostensible obstacle to their religious generosity. The monetary gifts which American Catholics bestow on the occasion of baptisms, funerals and "requiem" Masses are munificent compared to the paltry offerings made in Ireland. A vast majority of American churches were built within the memory of the present generation who contributed towards their erection. In Ireland, seventy-five per cent. of the inhabitants never witnessed the erection of their churches. Irish men and women who left the old "*Sod*" fifty or eighty years ago, can yet see the old chapels wherein their infant forms were *laved* in the waters of baptism and where they knelt and prayed in bye-gone days. The bones of those who built those grand old edifices are now resting in and around the ruins of old churches desecrated by Cromwell and his craven minions.

Hoping the reader will overlook this apparent digression, we will resume our comparison. In America, the poorest Catholic man or maid-servant either rents a seat in church or pays a small sum every Sunday. Church seats are never ren. d in Ireland for a year or fraction of a year; while only in Dublin, Cork and a few of the larger cities is any offering required for a special Sunday seat. In several dioceses of America, the Priests make quarterly, and in some places monthly collecting visitations throughout each parish, or else require monthly contributions in the church. Except the Xmas, Easter and Curates' collections, they seldom have other collections in Ireland.

Besides the general and munificent offerings of "All Souls' Day" the poorest family in America provide for a high Mass of "*requiem*" at the funeral of a deceased member. On such occasions in Ireland, there may be one or two *low* Masses offered. The Priests who attend funerals in Ireland are merely expected to wear a white linen sash and hat-band, while they accompany the funeral procession to the grave on an outside car. Again, in America, graves, cemetery lots and individual headstones are a source of considerable expense; in Ireland, one grave is generally made the repository of ancestry and posterity. While funerals in Ireland are less decorous and expensive, the adornment of cemeteries and graves, the numerous floral offerings and anniversary Masses for departed relatives in America have no equivalent in Ireland.

The substantial and financial contributions towards "*bazaars*," "*fairs*," "*picnics*," etc., in this country far exceed the receipts of similar devices in the Old country. Again, almost every Catholic church in America, including those of country villages, has a choir attached, whose organist and leading choristers receive a stipulated salary. Few, if any choirs are paid in Ireland, their services being usually volunteered. Indeed, if we except a few churches in Dublin, Cork and Belfast, solemn high Masses are never celebrated on Sundays or other days except on the occurrence of a special feast, whilst high Masses or *Missae cantatae* are never heard, low Masses being ordinarily substituted.

As we have already insinuated, churches, schools, convents and parsonages in America are continually being built, often before the ground on which they stand has been released of debt. The Pastor must borrow from a bank or some other influential corporation, whilst the poor parishioners have to ward off the foreclosure of mortgage by liberal, and often strained contributions. Irish Priests and Nuns who make a tour through the States in quest of contributions or send out numerous bazaar tickets, (a practice discouraged by the late Plenary Council of Baltimore), will be surprised and sorry to learn that some American Priests and Nuns have to contend not only against monetary embarrassment, but financial ruin.

We shall conclude our *relative* comparisons by adding that benevolent, total abstinence and religious societies for both sexes are more numerous and better organized in America than in Ireland.

AN APOLOGY.

IF, in the preceding pages, we have said things uncomplimentary to the present inhabitants of Ireland, we would make amends by reminding the reader that the peoples of other countries have social and religious defects, perhaps, more numerous and reprehensible. As a parent reveals greater wisdom and love by holding out for their inspection, the faults and foibles of his children, so we respectfully declare that the desire to render the people still more perfect has been the sole motive for our exposing their domestic habits to the gaze of the American public.

We are now pleased to concede to the Irish people, both of the present day and of all christian ages, the unstinted praise due their manifold virtues, especially their inflexible adherence to the Catholic religion. The late venerable Pope Pius IX said of them: "They are a brave, generous and Catholic people."

The Irish may truly be called a godly people; the worship of God is interwoven with their daily actions and ordinary conversation. No visitor will enter a house without saying "God bless, or God save all here;" the plowman, the spadesman, the harvester, and the "young maid milking her cow" are invariably blessed by the passer-by, and the salute politely returned—"God speed or bless you kindly, Sir or Madam." Tradesmen of every profession would consider themselves slighted, if not insulted, were an adult to omit this benedictive salute while passing by their work. It would be a breach of reciprocal courtesy to notice a child's physical or social qualities without a blessing. The writer can never forget how distressed a young Irish mother was when an Englishman referred to the beautiful child she held in her arms, without calling God to "bless" it. Even in epistolary correspondence, the same spirit prevails. Few letters are sent across the Atlantic from Ireland without a father's or mother's blessing and the writer's request for a remembrance in prayer. It would be reputed almost a sacrilege to mention a deceased person's name without saying "God have mercy, or God rest his or her soul."

With all our vaunted progress in etiquette and belles-letters, it must be admitted that the Irish form of salutation, chiefly common amongst the peasantry is less *material*, more christian than the American "How d' you do?" "So so," "Quite well, thank you," etc. The salutation of two persons meeting in Ireland would be considered abnormal if God's name were not hallowed in every reference to the day or night, the weather or condition of health.

While sojourning in Ireland a stranger would imagine he was living amid a patriarchal people who extolled God's name in all his works. The Irish peasantry not only observe the *spirit* but the *letter* of King David's psalter,* praising God for sun and moon, heat and cold, rain and drought."

The people are so thoroughly Catholic that they regard it a most grievous misfortune to omit or to be late for Mass on Sundays. Hence, over morass and mount-

---

* Laudate Dominum sol et lumen, etc. (Ps. 148).

ain, the young as also the old men and women (some beyond three score and ten) may be seen in the chapel (frequently fasting) after having *walked* a distance of *five* and often *seven* miles from their homes, regarding rain, heat or cold an insufficient excuse for their absence. Their manner of worship is awe-inspiring.

"In an Irish peasant congregation," says the popular authoress, Miss Banim, "there is a simplicity of devotion; an entire self-forgetfulness—a letting the entire soul and every thought show itself in the face and attitude. They seem to realize the solemnity of the words of Holy Writ: 'This is an awful place, the house of God.' Everything else is forgotten but God whom they desire to adore and to whom they offer every petition and expose every want. Here an old man kneels, his hands clasped on the crook of his stick, his chin resting on the folded hands, his eyes immovably fixed on the face of the Priest whose every movement and prayer he seems to comprehend; near him a woman prays in the reverential eastern attitude, the forehead touching the ground; beside this hooded figure, another woman prays half aloud, the arms extended in the form of a cross, reminding one of Josue whose prayers were heard only as long as his arms were extended in this attitude of supplication."

We locate France, Germany, Italy, Poland, Portugal and Spain in religious as well as alphabetical order by placing ERIN before them all in the catalogue of Catholicism. No other nation has suffered so much for conscience sake, or has been so cruelly and unjustly persecuted for its faith. When England and Scotland abandoned their ancestral faith, and espoused the cause of King Henry VIII, constituting himself head of the

English Church, with the design of repudiating his lawful wife, Queen Catharine of Arragon, Ireland assuming her native chivalry, espoused the forlorn cause of the British Queen and persistently maintained her adherence to the Papacy. The whole history of Irish persecution, emigration, poverty and national ostracism might be said to have emanated from her chivalric defence of womankind and her profession of Catholicity. Allurements, fortified by all the subtle wiles that craft and mammon could devise, were held out to proselytize the insolvent peasantry; the hungry were bribed with beef, bread and broth; the naked, with blankets, *breatheens* and brogues. Cromwell, in the fever of his exterminating wrath cried out: "To Hell or to Connaught." But Cromwell's official successors, including the present Prime Minister of England, (Lord Salisbury), grudge the people the poor homes they selected in Connaught. Their cry now is, "To Hell or to America." Hence, ocean steamers, the whole year round, are laden with human freight from every Irish port.

Political preferment is as difficult at present as it was in the days of Old King Harry. In truth, it seems as if "*Old Harry*" of another realm was the chief ruler in Ireland still.

The qualifications of an Irishman must be magnified by a powerful British microscope before they can be classified with those of an English aspirant. There are four qualities especially remarkable in the character of the Irish people, viz: Their devotion to the Blessed Virgin, their respect for the Priesthood, their veneration of St. Patrick, and their love and practice of holy purity. The Virgin's name and attributes are hallowed throughout the land; shrines and altars are everywhere dedicated to her; in every family, the female favorite is called after the Virgin, Mary.* Almost every household in Ireland recite the rosary before retiring to rest at night; whilst young, and especially old men and women remain for hours on Sundays with upturned eyes and clasped hands, offering prayers before the image of the Mother of God; the itinerant mendicant always solicits alms in the names of Jesus and Mary; every paternal and maternal blessing is besought and imparted in the name of the Father, Son and Holy Ghost and the Virgin Mary. A large majority of the cathedral churches and convents of Ireland are named after the Virgin or dedicated under the auspices of some of her saintly attributes.

The next characteristic feature of the Irish people, their respect for the Priesthood, is proverbial. *Soggart Aroon*† is one of the most endearing expressions of the Celtic tongue. The proud aristocrat, the penniless bankrupt, rich and poor, young and old, unbosom to him their most secret thoughts and actions. A gentle wave of the Priest's hand is more efficient in suppressing popular tumult than a regiment of constablery. The Catholic who fails to respect the Priest is looked upon as a *shoneen* on the verge of apostasy.

This respect will appear quite natural when we consider that the Priests always stood by the people and

---

* " Is thy name Mary, maiden fair?
　Such should, methinks, its music be;
　The sweetest names that mortals bear,
　　Were best befitting thee.
　　　　　　—O. W. Holmes.

† Sagart arûn (Priest dear) rendered into verse by John Banim.

administered to their spiritual and temporal wants even when their oppressors forced them to flee to the mountains, forests and caverns. "The Catholic Priests," writes Justin MacCarthy, "braved shame and persecution and death in their unswerving allegiance to their scattered flocks." When no Catholic might open a school, the Priests established what were known as "*hedge schools.*" By the roadside, and by the hillside, in ditches and behind hedges, the children of the people cowered about their pastors, eagerly striving to attain that knowledge which the harsh laws denied them.

"The Catholic clergy," continues the same author, "came fearlessly to the front; many of the little bands of rebels who endeavored to resist their oppressors were led into action by the Priests; Father Michael Murphy, Father Philip Roche and Father John Murphy, (who died on the gallows), were amongst the bravest and ablest of the revolutionary leaders. In the preceding pages, we have shown where the Irish Bishops and Priests of the present day are amongst the most uncompromising promoters of the national cause.†

The third religious feature of the Irish character, the veneration of St. Patrick, is international.

While other nations have lost respect for their patron Saints, Ireland remained unchanged. Although St.

---

† Mr. Wm. O'Brien, M. P., in a speech delivered at Naul, Co. Dublin, (Feb. 6. 1890) said:—I will ask your leave to say one word in support of the vote of thanks to your *soggarth aroon*, Father Dunphy. I must say that his pleasant face here to-day has made me forget that the sun is not shining (laughter). . . . . There is no nobler chapter in Irish history than the union of priests and people (cheers). They fought together in hard times and they won together. We fight together now, and we will win together too (loud cheers).

James is the Apostle of Spain, yet meet with a Spaniard in any country on St. James' day, his step is not more elastic, his eye is not brighter than usual—he fails to celebrate his national feast; for him, it is an ordinary day. Saints Peter and Paul are the Patrons of Rome, where they received the palm of martyrdom; yet the Roman laity do not solemnize their national feast-day (29th June). St. Remi baptized Clovis, the founder of the Frankish monarchy; yet there are thousands of Frenchmen who do not know the name of their national Saint.

But Ireland, with a chronicle of heroic deeds sufficient to illuminate the brighest pages of Continental history—she, in the days of her bondage as in the days of her freedom, will recognize no other national feast besides St. Patrick's. It is a holiday of obligation throughout the entire island. On this day, Ireland's sons and fair daughters congregate at their festive reunions, not only in Ireland, but on the plains watered by the Yellowstone, the Columbia and the Nile.

The fourth and chief characteristic feature of the Irish nation is the acknowledged purity of its people.

It is a significant fact, indicative of Irish purity, that children born of wedlock in Ireland out-number those of any other European country.

The statistics of illegitimacy and abortion in England, Scotland, Germany and France are disreputable compared with the isolated cases reported for Ireland; whilst divorce statistics are still more divergent.

The State of Maine, U. S., (in 1882), with a population of 660,000, reported 587 divorces; whilst Ireland, having in the same year a population of 5,340,000, recorded but six divorces.*

In Warner's History of Ireland (Book I., c. 10), we read that a princely-born young lady, adorned with jewels and costly raiment, undertook alone a journey from one end of the kingdom to the other.† This event has been versified by the poet Moore :

> "Rich and rare were the gems she wore
> And a bright gold ring on her wand she bore;
> But Oh! her beauty was far beyond
> Her sparkling gems and snow-white wand.
>
> Lady, dost thou not fear to stray
> Through this lone and bleak way?
> Are Erin's sons so good or so cold
> As not to be tempted by woman or gold?
>
> Sir Knight, I feel not the least alarm;
> No son of Erin will offer me harm;
> For altho' they love woman and golden store,
> Sir Knight, they love honor and virtue more.
>
> On she went, and her maiden smile
> In safety lighted her 'round the Green Isle,
> And blessed forever was she who relied
> On Erin's honor and Erin's pride."

---

* The historian Winterer, in his book on German Socialism furnishes the following statistics:—

In 1882 there were 22 divorces for every 10,000 marriages in England.

In 1882 there were 35 divorces for every 10,000 marriages in Germany.

In 1882 there were 75 divorces for every 10,000 marriages in France.

In 1882 there were 3 divorces for every 10,000 marriages in Ireland.

Illinois records 32,360 divorces in 20 years, or one divorce for every nine marriages Maine, one divorce for every ten marriages; New Hampshire, one in eleven; Rhode Island, one in ten; Vermont, one in ten. If the Catholics in these States were excluded, the proportion would be much greater.

† This event took place during the reign of Brian Boru, (1001 A. D).

CONCLUSION.

WE are pleased to affirm that the present agrarian and political aspect of Ireland is most encouraging, and to predict that the country will never again be reduced to its former serfdom. In the language of Dr. MacCarthy, (Bishop of Cloyne·), "The time for the high-handed exercise of landlord power has now happily passed away—and passed away, never to return." Whilst the Irish Episcopate and Clergy are unanimous with the laity in their demands for Home Rule, the English and Scotch people were never so favorably disposed. Not only the Irish Representatives, but the entire Liberal party, including some of the leading minds of the British Empire, advocate autonomy for Ireland.*

It is an unfounded aspersion to assert or insinuate that the Irsh are naturally disunited or disloyal. It is true, they are indisposed, or if you will call it *disloyal*, towards the alleged "*Union*" that has robbed them of their lands, language and liberty. In every country, the Irish are law-abiding and benevolent citizens.† No

---

* In 1887, out of a total of 670 members of the House of Commons, 313 were in favor of Home Rule.

† American history relates that Lord Howe, the English Admiral, attempted to bribe an Irishman, Commodore John Barry (the father of the American Navy). He offered him 15,000 guineas and the command of a British ship if he would desert and join the English forces. He boldly replied:—"I would not for the value or command of the whole British Navy, abandon the cause of my country."

other nation of the globe has a right to adjudicate this question before America, as no other rules such a mighty body of our countrymen. On the other side of the Atlantic, we only see the little island of old Ireland with a sparse population, coerced and oppressed by vicious laws and rapacious landlords ; but here, we have the great continent of YOUNG IRELAND with more than ten million inhabitants, vigorous, prosperous and free.

Our harbors are, as they have ever been, open to welcome the Exile of Erin.

Throughout the extent of this mighty continent, in the forests and prairies, as well as on the cultivated banks of the Mississippi, Ohio and Hudson are erected the prosperous homes of those whose infant forms were baptized in the crystal waters of the Shannon, the Lee, the Liffey and the Avoca ; or whose agile limbs sported on the mossy banks of the Barrow, the Nore, the Bann and the Suir. America sympathizes with the old land of the Celts ; whilst she blushes at her misdeeds and winces at her oppression, she smiles at her success and her forbearance.

Ever since the days of the revolution, Irish records are interwoven with American history ; Irish heads and hands were devoted to the service of our Government, Army and Navy. Irishmen fought for America in her darkest hours, struggled with her in her political, physical and financial embarrassments, and the bones of her bravest sons, named and nameless, repose in her most blood-stained battlefields. Hence, at all times, but more especially at the present, American sentiment upholds the Irish cause. Not only tens of thousands, but millions and tens of millions of the dauntless sons and fair daughters of young America yearn and pray for

Ireland's prosperity. And should Ireland obtain Home Rule and her green flag be raised once again from the Saxon dust, a mighty shout of joy would resound throughout our broad States and Territories, so loud and thrilling that it would almost be heard in old Ireland itself.

As the first American flag was wrought by the fair hands of an Irish-American lady, so in every State of this glorious and prosperous country are maidens anxious to weave another liberty banner emblazoned with the Sun-burst, Harp and Shamrock.

We hope and pray that the day may not be far distant when the GREEN FLAG shall proudly float over the Parliament House and Legislative Halls of our native land.

ERIN MY COUNTRY.

"Dear Erin my country, with rapture I love thee,
    And deep are my longings to see thee once more;
No land in this green-covered earth is above thee;
    No coast can compare with thy sea-beaten shore.

Thy greenest of bosoms, I'd make my last pillow,
    On thy silken-moss'd banks weave a chaplet of green;
To garland my temple and sleep 'neath the willow
    That grows by the cot where I took my first being.

Thy Shamrock, than Emerald is greener and dearer,
    And sparkling like diamonds, the rivers unfold;
No skies to my vision are lovelier, clearer,
    Thy sun-lighted mountains look richer than gold.

In spirit I roam o'er thy hoary-peaked mountains,
    And watch the gay lark pour his song to the skies,
And wander 'mid streamlet or rippling fountain
    'Till memory comes rushing with rain to my eyes.

Again, the rich sunlight makes sport with thy waters,
    And pay back its glances with bright winning smiles;
Thy valorous sons, and thy beautiful daughters
    Proclaim thee their goddess, the Queen of the Isles."

www.ingramcontent.com/pod-product-compliance
Lightning Source LLC
Chambersburg PA
CBHW020827190426
43197CB00037B/727